A History of

SHOPS & SHOPPING

in Scotland

Sharon Barron

cilips

Published by The Chartered Institute of Library and
Information Professionals in Scotland • 2002

1st Floor Building C,
Brandon Gate,
Leechlee Road,
Hamilton ML3 6AU

ISBN 0 954116011

Designed by GSB (Edinburgh).
Printed by Nevisprint, Fort William, Scotland.

For Laurence

"The car, the furniture, the wife, the children - everything has to be disposable. Because you see the main thing today is - shopping. Years ago a person, he was unhappy, didn't know what to do with himself - he'd go to church, start a revolution - something. Today you're unhappy? Can't figure it out? What is the salvation? Go shopping."

Arthur Miller. The Price, 1, 1968

Contents

List of Illustrations

Every effort has been made to seek the permission of copyright holders to reproduce the photographs used in this publication. We are most grateful to those copyright holders who gave permission for the following illustrations to be used.

Acknowledgements

I received a great deal of help from librarians all over Scotland and am most grateful to them all. I would like to thank the following especially for their patience and co-operation

Sheila Millar, Midlothian Council
Eileen Moran, Dundee City Council
M. Sybil Cavanagh, West Lothian Council
Catherine Taylor, Aberdeen City Council
Eleanor Harris, Argyll and Bute Council
Helen Darling, Scottish Borders Council
Maud Devine, East Renfrewshire Council
Ian Nelson, Edinburgh City Council
Enda Ryan, Glasgow City Council
Tricia Burke, Renfrewshire Council
Phil Astley and Sweyn Johnston, Orkney Islands Council
David Young, South Lanarkshire Council

Grateful thanks are due to Conal Anderson of SCRAN for his help and to Helen Young of the People's Story, Edinburgh, for permission to access the People's Story Oral History Archive and to quote from it in Chapter 7. I have to extend thanks also to Michael and Sandra Bullough of McEwen's of Perth, Sarah Emslie of Jenners and Yvonne Smith of Eric N Smith for their co-operation. I have been fortunate in the willingness of many to share recollections and observations with me and I would like to record my gratitude in particular to Helene Wolf, Joan Sellyn, Linda and Kenny Davidson, Kitty Harris, Lorraine MacCuish, Jenny Goldberg, Daniel Barron and Esther Petkus for informative and stimulating discussion. Thanks too to Alan Reid and Brian Osborne for comment on the manuscript and to Susannah Cohen for all her help and for her unstinting encouragement.

Malcolm III

Chapter 1

In the beginning

In the middle of the eleventh century, Queen Margaret of Scotland, the wife of Malcolm III, catapulted shopping to the forefront of Scotland's agenda. Even before the various states of the northern part of Britain were forged into a single kingdom, there is evidence that there had been international trading links between Scotland and the continent. Archaeological evidence points to a former Viking trading settlement at Whithorn and to trading networks between Scotland, the west coast of Ireland and France from as early as the late sixth century, for the supply of goods such as wine, olive oil, glass and spices. But it was not until the formidable and stylish Queen Margaret stepped in that things began to speed up.

Before becoming King of Scots in 1058, Malcolm III had spent many years exiled in England and Normandy. His second wife, Margaret, was a Saxon princess and she too had been exiled from her country, having been born and brought up in Hungary. Margaret was extremely devout and, as Queen of Scotland, she involved herself in church reforms and was responsible for the introduction of the Benedictine order to Scotland. Her piety was sufficiently remarkable that she was canonised in 1250. However, Margaret's concerns were not entirely confined to the spiritual. Malcolm and Margaret were both used to a certain degree of elegance and elegance was something that was sadly lacking at the Scottish court. Margaret embarked on a makeover of epic proportions. She introduced her courtiers to fine clothes, jewellery and works of art and they rather enjoyed it. Indeed, they went a step further and began to adopt many of the more sophisticated manners and customs of the English and

St Margaret

continental nobility as well. In the book that he wrote about her life and work, Margaret's confessor, Turgot, described the transformation process:

> The queen, a noble gem of royal race, much more ennobled the splendour of her husband's kingly magnificence, and contributed no little glory and grandeur to the entire nobility of the realm and their retainers. It was due to her that the merchants who came by land and sea, by various countries, brought along with them for sale different kinds of precious wares, which until then were unknown in Scotland. And it was at her instigation that the natives of Scotland purchased from these traders clothing of various colours, with ornaments to wear, so that from this period, through her suggestion, new costumes of different fashions were adopted, the elegance of which made the wearers appear like a new race of beings.

Margaret's initiative may well have prompted St Godric to travel to Scotland for the first time. St Godric began his working life as a pedlar. He used to carry his wares all the way from his native Lincolnshire to St Andrews in Scotland. Godric prospered and he was able in time to buy a share in a sailing ship that enabled him to sail to Europe to seek out interesting new stock. It also allowed him to ply his trade at home in somewhat grander style. He no longer had to trudge the inland byways. He could now take a more leisurely route and sail to Scotland in style. His life changed completely when he visited Lindisfarne and came under the influence of St Cuthbert. Although he was still a successful businessman, Godric became well known for his new-found piety. He was scrupulous in his devotions and made countless pilgrimages throughout his working life. In due course Godric gave up business altogether and distributed his wealth and possessions amongst the poor. He went to live at Finchale near Durham where he adopted the life of a religious hermit. Like Queen Margaret, Godric was eventually declared a saint and Finchale went on to become the site of a Benedictine priory.

Malcolm and Margaret's youngest son, David I, succeeded to the throne of Scotland in 1124, on the death of his elder brother. David undertook a revolution that changed the economic landscape of Scotland completely. He put into place an infrastructure that gave Scotland places that were licensed for trading, encouraged people to trade and introduced coinage with which trade could be conducted.

David was only nine years old when his parents died and he was sent to live in England, where his sister, Matilda, was married to the King, Henry I. He became a member of the royal household and attained considerable wealth and influence when he married a rich Norman-English widow. David's rule of Scotland during almost three decades was heavily influenced by his formative years in England. He was of the firm opinion that he would bring more stability to Scotland if he adopted the

Anglo-Norman model of government. To this end and to ensure that he had a strong military and administrative support base, he granted estates in Scotland to a number of Anglo-Norman lords. He also followed in his mother's footsteps and encouraged the foundation of new monasteries and abbeys, recognising that they too would contribute to order and prosperity in Scotland.

In a deliberate attempt to consolidate his own position and to give his commercial initiative the best possible chance of success, David established many of the earliest burghs in areas that had been settled by the Norman lords who had accompanied him from England. Others, with natural geographical advantages such as a sheltered harbour, almost selected themselves; Roxburgh and Berwick-upon-Tweed had achieved *de facto* burgh status even before David came to the throne. In the very first year of his reign, David created nine royal burghs: Dunfermline, Aberdeen, Perth, Stirling, Edinburgh, Renfrew, Rutherglen, Peebles and Hamilton. In broad terms, a burgh was a town or settlement that had been given the right to become a trading centre. When a town or settlement was given the status of burgh, a set of legal rights and privileges was conferred upon it by the crown that had mainly, although not entirely, to do with trade. In return for such benefits, taxes were imposed upon the burgh and taxes accrued in this way soon became a major source of royal revenue.

Some seventy royal burghs were created in Scotland by 1707. In the first instance the monarch issued a verbal proclamation. This was followed by the gift of a written charter that set out the privileges and responsibilities conferred on the burgh and its burgesses. All of the burgh charters were substantially the same, although they varied slightly in detail to allow for local circumstances.

Once the burgh system was in place, the people of Scotland had somewhere to go shopping. Trading outside the network of chartered burghs was illegal; trading inside the burghs was quite legal and was also positively encouraged. As a result, some burghs attracted merchants and skilled craftsmen from other parts of Scotland, England and even overseas, from places like the Low Countries, Germany and France. The new settlers recognised the commercial opportunities that the burghs offered. Burghs were given the right to hold weekly markets and annual fairs. The number of fairs that a burgh was entitled to hold was detailed in its royal charter. Royal burghs also had the right to trade overseas and to sell goods imported from abroad. The exclusive rights of burghs persisted for much longer in Scotland than they did in England. To a very great extent, the burghs retained their monopoly of trade until about the latter half of the seventeenth century, by which time an increasing number of licences were being issued for fairs and markets to be held at other locations. Surprisingly, even though the system was so blatantly restrictive, the burghs' monopoly of trade was not without advantage to the consumer. Strenuous effort was made to ensure that goods were presented for sale without undue profiteering and the regulations against 'regrating', buying to sell at a profit, and 'forestalling', the purchasing of goods before they were offered publicly for sale, were enforced with great strictness.

There were three categories of burgh. A royal burgh received its charter directly from the king. Some feudal lords, heads of religious houses, and bishops were empowered by the king to create burghs themselves. These had a somewhat lesser status and were known as 'burghs of barony and regality'. The burgesses of these burghs paid their sales taxes to their feudal lord rather than to the king. On the face of it therefore, each time that a king sanctioned the creation of a burgh of barony rather than a royal burgh, he was making an extraordinarily generous gesture. In fact,

Kirkcudbright Tolbooth

the crown did very well out of the burghs of barony. Financially, the crown still gained, because the income that the feudal lord accrued from the burgesses was subject to tax; politically, the crown gained as well, because a feudal lord was indebted to the king for the favour that had been bestowed upon him. While burghs of barony enjoyed many of the privileges of royal burghs, the royal burghs held on to their exclusive right to overseas trade until 1672. As well as the burghs of barony, a number of ecclesiastical burghs were created. These were almost identical to the burghs of barony, but they had an ecclesiastical rather than a baronial overlord. After a period of time, a number of burghs of barony and ecclesiastical burghs were adopted as royal burghs.

Aberdeen's harbour gave it a tremendous natural advantage as a domestic and international trading centre and it was one of the first royal burghs to be created. A charter of 1273 affirmed Aberdeen's right to hold a general market each week in the Castlegate, the main street of the burgh. This was also the location of Aberdeen's tolbooth and everything that was sold in the town had to be brought to the tolbooth to be assessed for taxation purposes.

Aberdeen was a good place to go shopping. Its history is very well documented and the records show that the burgh council and its magistrates were vigilant in their attempts to keep the price and quality of everyday necessities under control. They suffered one all too conspicuous failure nevertheless: they proved quite unequal to the task of regulating the sale of fish at the seashore. In all other respects, they were more successful. In the 1440s the price of wool was set by the authorities at a maximum of five shillings a stone and the price of ale set variously at two pence and four pence a gallon. There was a lengthy period of inflation between 1435 and 1531 and the records reveal that bread doubled in price and mutton went up by two and a quarter times between these years. Butchers and bakers were fined for selling at other than the official market price. The going price for a boll of corn and a boll of malt was announced regularly: in the late fourteenth century this ranged from three shillings to four shillings for corn and two shillings and eight pence to four shillings for malt.

The burgesses battled constantly to prevent forestalling. Rural tanners were particularly guilty of this misdemeanour and were frequently found to have bought hides before they had been offered on the open market. Sometimes burgesses themselves were tempted to break the rules and in 1438 five of them were found guilty of forestalling. Four received swingeing fines of twenty shillings each, although one escaped with a lesser fine of four shillings. The regulations stated that, except for salt and herring, all goods brought in by ship had to be sold on land and displayed for all to see. Nevertheless, infringement was rife. Anyone who was not a burgess had to pay a fee to sell their goods at the market: an uncovered booth cost a farthing and a covered booth a halfpenny and many thought it worth the risk to try to evade the cost. In 1399 a ship's master stood accused of selling apples and pears straight from his ship, instead of taking them to market. However, the burgh council was not inflexible. There was a severe shortage of food in Aberdeen during the winter of 1509 and the council realised that they would need to act decisively to prevent disaster. As a temporary measure, all tax and burgh regulations were waived in an attempt to encourage anyone who had any food to sell to bring it to Aberdeen's market.

Inveraray's charter was granted in 1474, when King James III 'for his singular favour toward Colin, Earl of Ergile, Lord Campbell and Lorne, Master of his Household, and for the Earl's gratuitous and faithful services to the King's late father and to himself' declared Inveraray a free burgh of barony. The Earl of Argyll was the feudal lord of the farming community around Inveraray. As such, he had the right to appoint the new burgh council office bearers and to preside over the burgh court. The charter granted Inveraray a weekly Saturday market and two annual fairs and the small settlement had to establish a tollhouse where tolls could be collected on the goods that were to be sold on these occasions. Typically, these included wool, cheese, feathers, eggs, salmon, milk and animal skins. Inveraray's annual fairs were set for 29th September, which was the Feast of St Michael the Archangel, and on 16th May, the Feast of St Brandan, and for the eight days that followed both celebrations.

In 1554 and again in 1572, there were indications given that Inveraray might become a royal burgh, although its translation did not actually take place until 1648. On its official enrolment as a royal burgh in 1649, the commissioner for the Burgh of Dumbarton entered a caveat that the new royal burgh should not prejudice the liberty of the Burgh of Dumbarton. As more and more burghs were created, established burghs, such as Dumbarton, became extremely anxious to safeguard their longstanding monopoly of local trade against their upstart neighbours.

A royal charter was issued to the Abbot and Monastery of Culross on 14th April 1490 for the creation of the Burgh of Culross. The new burgh was granted a weekly market on a Sunday and an annual fair on 21st September, the Feast of Saint Matthew. In 1588, James VI granted Culross a royal charter that gave a weekly market on a Tuesday and an annual fair that began with the Feast of St Martin's. In 1592, when Culross became a royal burgh, a further charter gave a market day on Saturday and entitled the burgh to two fairs, one of which was to be held on 1st July, the Festival of St Serf (or St Servan). The Festival of St Serf was celebrated with great gusto and, by the end of the eighteenth century, the *Statistical Account of Scotland, 1791-1799*, records that the festivities included:

> a variety of ceremonies, particularly parading the streets and environs of the town very early in the morning, with large branches of birch and other trees in their foliage, accompanied with drums and other musical instruments, adorning the cross and another public place called the *Tron*,

with a great profusion and variety of flowers, formed into different devices, and spending the day in festivity and mirth.

This traditional celebration was maintained well into the nineteenth century, although by then the date of the fair had been changed to 4th June, the birthday of George III.

The creation of the burghs was not quite enough. David knew that the absence of coinage was a continuing barrier to the development of trade in Scotland. Before he ordered the minting of Scottish coins, trade was conducted largely by means of barter, although, in the case of international trade at least, it is likely that some foreign currency was used as well. In 1136, David went to the support of his niece, Matilda, who was fighting for the English crown. He invaded northern England and took possession of Carlisle. There was a royal mint in Carlisle that Stephen of England had been using for his own coinage. David quickly appropriated this mint and used it to strike the first Scottish coins. Once production moved to Scotland, there was no single Scottish mint. Instead, a total of sixteen different mints were established in locations throughout the country. This number was slowly reduced as coins of different denominations were introduced, until eventually only the Edinburgh mint was operational. It has been estimated that about forty million pennies were in circulation by 1280 when the minting of specific halfpenny and farthing coins began. Until this time, the original silver pennies had simply been clipped to make halfpennies and farthings. In due course, yet more coins of differing values were added, such as the groat, a large silver coin with a value of four pence, the bodle, or hard-head, a copper coin that was worth two pence, and the bawbee. The bawbee was a base metal coin that is thought to have got its wonderful name from Alexander Orrock, the Laird of Sillebawby, who was appointed Master of the Mint in 1538 when the coin was introduced. It was originally valued at three and then later at six pence Scots, but it was only worth one halfpenny in English money. The Act of Union brought about a uniformity of coinage, weights and measures to Scotland and England and there were no coins minted in Edinburgh after 1709, although the old Scottish coins remained in circulation for some considerable time.

There were still occasional hiccups in the supply of coins. During the late eighteenth and early nineteenth centuries there was a severe

The obverse of a Henry, Earl of Northumberland silver penny, minted at Carlisle between 1136 and 1152

shortage of small denomination legal tender because of a steep rise in demand. An increasing number of coins was needed to pay the wages of those who had gone to work in the new manufacturing industries. Many businesses dealt with the problem by issuing their own trade tokens.

Coats farthing

The Coats Farthing is just one of the very many trade tokens that were issued in the late eighteenth and nineteenth centuries. Jervis Coats, a member of the famous Paisley textile family, worked originally as a handloom weaver, but had to give up weaving in 1812 at the age of forty because his eyesight had become so poor. He turned instead to grocery and opened a shop with his brother. Unfortunately, there was an unusually high proportion of counterfeit change in circulation at this time and his customers soon realised that, because of his poor eyesight, Jervis was unable to spot the fakes. A farthing was still worth something in those days. You could buy a farthing candle or a farthing's worth of commodities such as tea, sugar and sweets, and the temptation to pass on a counterfeit coin was obviously too great for some of Jervis's customers to withstand. His shop was just the place to palm off any counterfeit money that you had been given. It was spoken of as 'the best in the town for getting full value for bad bawbees'. At the end of each day's trading, Jervis would get someone else to go through his takings and abstract any false coins. He stored these counterfeits until he had accumulated quite a collection. He then obtained permission to have them converted into trade tokens that would be worth a farthing. Jervis Coats was a ham curer as well as a grocer and he chose a representation of a ham for the face of his tokens. It is estimated that he had 20,000 of these farthings struck and they were a wonderful advertisement for his shop, which continued to be listed in various editions of the *Paisley Trade Directory* from 1812 until 1935.

Chapter 2

Traders, markets and fairs

Within the burghs, goods were sold at markets and fairs. The development of the modern shop was very gradual indeed and it was not until the end of the sixteenth century that the first permanent booths were built for retailing. At the medieval markets and fairs, people traded from carts, trays and tables; some people simply laid out their goods on the ground. The weekly burgh markets were routine affairs. They gave local people the opportunity to buy and sell everyday goods on a regular basis. A fair was rather more of an occasion. It was a boisterous blend of commerce, entertainment and celebration that attracted visitors from well beyond the immediate vicinity of a burgh. Trading restrictions were fewer and less strictly applied at fairs than at markets and, as a result, they attracted traders from all over Scotland and even from abroad. There were many itinerant traders. Pedlars roamed the countryside, visiting people in their homes and vying with local traders for custom at markets and fairs.

Chief among the citizens of a burgh were its burgesses. Most men of property became burgesses and they alone had the right to trade within the burgh without restriction. The commercial domination of the burgesses often extended beyond the nucleus of the burgh itself to include the surrounding areas. These were known as the burgh's 'liberty' and, as the burghs proliferated, so did the arguments over liberty boundaries and jurisdiction. Anyone from within the liberty area of a burgh wanting to sell produce or goods was only allowed to do so at that burgh's market where the appropriate duties and market fees would be applied. The burgesses used this revenue to defray the burden of royal taxation that was imposed upon them. In a royal charter of 1364, David II confirmed the rights of burgesses to trade within their own liberties, but stipulated that before they could trade in the liberties of any other burgh they must first obtain a licence. Notwithstanding that, the burgesses of some royal burghs were granted exemption from tolls throughout the kingdom in an endeavour to improve the economic viability of national and international trading. When Arbroath became a royal burgh in 1599, its burgesses were granted this particular privilege. The burgesses of a burgh were given the right to elect the burgh's council and its magistrates. The burgh administration had a duty to uphold the laws of the land, but was autonomous in local matters. Together, council and judiciary could establish and apply local rules and regulations and punish those who infringed them. The administration could even control access to the burgh, by placing a guard on the main entry and exit points and locking the gates of the town at night.

Within burgh society, there was a clear division of the population into burgesses and non-burgesses and there was a further subdivision of merchants and craftsmen into various guilds. The guild system offered a limited opportunity for social advancement as an apprentice to a burgess stood a fair chance of achieving his master's status in time. There were guilds in most countries of Europe during the middle ages. A guild was a special-interest association that served a dual purpose. The main purpose of the guild was to protect and further the professional interests of its members, but the guild also provided an embryonic social service for its members. Guilds assumed responsibility for any of their members who fell on hard times and for their dependents if they were left in need. The two types of guild, the merchant guild and the craft or trade guild did not always coexist comfortably. Many merchants believed that they were a cut above the craftsmen and certainly it was more usual for merchants to be in the majority on the town council and amongst high office bearers. However, it was the craftsmen who produced the goods and the merchants could not afford to alienate them; craft guilds controlled production and training in their particular sector and could exercise considerable power. There was no uniform pattern to the formation of guilds; however, there had to be enough potential members within any one burgh for the formation of a guild to be feasible, and a few towns did not have them at all. In time, some guilds came to be recognised formally by the crown.

One such, the Incorporation of Goldsmiths of the City of Edinburgh, has a venerable history. It was established in the early fifteenth century to protect the interests of the goldsmiths, silversmiths and jewellers in the city and to regulate the craftsmanship of its members. It was not unusual for goldsmiths in the smaller burghs to be members of a less specialised Incorporation of Hammermen, but there had long been a concentration of goldsmiths living and working in Edinburgh and a separate association was fully viable. From 1457, Scottish goldsmiths were obliged to stamp their identifying mark on the goods that they produced and have the quality of their metal tested. The deacon of the guild was given the responsibility of assaying and marking the goldsmiths' work. If it passed muster, it was given two further stamps: the mark of the deacon and the mark of the town in which it was made. Once an item was fully hallmarked, the customer could be confident of its quality. The Incorporation of Goldsmiths of the City of Edinburgh has been guaranteeing the quality of its members' work since the fifteenth century and is justly proud of its position as the oldest consumer protection group in Scotland. The Incorporation was granted a royal charter by King James VII & II in 1687 and approximately one hundred years later, in 1784, it became responsible for assaying and marking all gold and silver goods made in Scotland. From 1819 to 1964, this task was undertaken jointly with an assay office in Glasgow.

George Heriot

George Heriot was a member of the Incorporation of Goldsmiths of the City of Edinburgh in the sixteenth century. His vast fortune earned him the sobriquet of Jinglin' Geordie. He was born in Edinburgh sometime around 1563. He was the eldest son of a large family descended from an old East Lothian family, the Heriots of Traboun. George Heriot's father was also a goldsmith and a deacon of the Incorporation of Goldsmiths. George followed in his father's footsteps and became a member of the Incorporation himself in 1588. Ten years later he became deacon of the Incorporation for the first time and he went on to become deacon on two further occasions. Like many of his fellow goldsmiths in Edinburgh at

Anne of Denmark

that time, George Heriot was a wealthy man and managed a highly successful business. He had sufficient funds to develop a second career as a moneylender.

In 1597, he was appointed goldsmith to Anne of Denmark, the wife of James VI. In 1601 he was made Royal Goldsmith to the king himself. As Royal Goldsmith, Heriot was charged with making and sourcing gold and silverwork and jewellery for the crown. There is little evidence that George Heriot undertook very much craftsmanship himself and certainly there are no surviving pieces bearing Heriot's mark. What we can be sure of, however, is that George Heriot was frequently called upon to bail out his royal master financially and, to all intents and purposes, he became the king's banker and pawnbroker. When James succeeded to the English throne and moved to London, George Heriot moved with him. This move brought him even greater prosperity, but those who stayed behind were not quite as lucky. In the wake of the Union and the removal of the court and the gentry to London, traders suffered from the imposition of new excise duties and a decline in the demand for luxury goods. Early in *The Heart of Midlothian*, Sir Walter Scott gave voice to their bitterness:

The inscription panel from the Preparatory School for George Heriot's Hospital School, Old Assembly Close, High Street, Edinburgh

"Weary on Lunnon and a' that e'er came out o't!" said Miss Grizell Damahoy, an ancient seamstress; "they hae taen awa our parliament, and they hae oppressed our trade. Our gentles will hardly allow that a Scots needle can sew ruffles on a sark, or lace on an overlay."

But, in London, Jinglin' Geordie just got richer and richer. George Heriot did not have any children of his own. After his death, his will revealed that he wanted his fortune to fund a school for the education of fatherless sons of freemen and burgesses of the City of Edinburgh. George Heriot's school, or 'Hospital' as it was then known, opened in 1659. It is now an independent co-educational school.

The earliest markets were like general stores. It was not until about the seventeenth century that the practice of having different market days, and possibly even different locations, for specific types of goods became more prevalent. By the nineteenth century, a large town might hold a number of distinct annual, weekly or daily markets. The entry for Aberdeen in the *New Statistical Account for Scotland*, 1845 notes that:

> There is a weekly market on Thursdays for meal, and on Fridays for grain, butcher-meat, and other provisions. Within the last few years several butchers' shops have been opened in the town, where a supply of meat may be obtained on any day of the week. There is a fish market daily, unless in tempestuous weather; and a supply of cured fish, including the well-known 'Findon Haddocks' may be had daily.
>
> A market for the sale of linen is held on the Green on the last Wednesday of April, and a wool market is held there in the last week of June, and the first two weeks of July, on Thursday and Friday.
>
> The timber-market for the sale of tubs and other wooden articles is held in the Castle Street on the last Wednesday in August.
>
> The feeing market for the hiring of farm-servants is held in the vicinity of the meal-market at Aberdeen, on the second Friday of May and November.
>
> Besides these markets held in Aberdeen, there are several markets for horses and cattle, held in the close vicinity of the town...

From this entry we can see that it was well into the nineteenth century before the people of Aberdeen could buy fresh meat on more than one day of the week and before shops really began to impact on the food trade of the markets. It was just at this time, when the number of shops was on the increase, that a brand new covered market was built in Aberdeen on the ancient Green. By 1910, Wallace & Co., family butchers based in the Market Hall, was advertising, 'Families waited on daily (if desired) for Orders.'

Timmer Market, despite its name, was really a fair. The exact origins of Aberdeen's Timmer Market are unknown. It is thought to date back to the thirteenth century, although it is not mentioned in local records until 1773. As its name would suggest, its main focus was wooden goods, but it specialised in late summer fruits as well. It also featured an unofficial but lively trade in contraband whisky. By the mid nineteenth century there were rumblings that the market was not what it used to be. In 1839, the local paper reported a shortage of juniper berries, or 'etnachs', much sought by 'economical housekeepers' to convert bad whisky into good gin, and in 1849 the paper's reporter bemoaned a general drop in standards:

> It is a yearly falling away. One looks in vain for the curious articles of home manufacture, or the antiquated-looking denizens of the hills with their wooden wares.

However, he noted with approval that the traditionally rowdy evening festivities had taken place without incident. The *Daily Journal* of 1911

Timmer Market, Castlegate, 1934

asserted that the market had so declined that it had become merely a rather inferior toy fair and a parody of its former self, but by 1919 the paper was less disapproving. After five years of war, the end was in sight and Aberdonians welcomed the excuse to party:

> Following precedent, the youngsters, and a good many of the older lads also, provided themselves with trumpets and horns, and gave the market its time honoured accompaniment of discordant sounds.

In 1926, there was a touch of the exotic about the market. For the very first time a group of Indian traders was in attendance. They returned the following year:

> It was a curious mixture of the old and the new to see a stall laden with spurtles, brose caps, and all the 'pre-historic' relics of handicraft in wood cheek by jowl with another containing all the silken products of the Orient, and with dusky, turbaned Indians as the grave and silent presiding stallites.

Timmer Market was moved from Castlegate to the new market site in 1935. Latterly it has moved back to its traditional location and stallholders have been encouraged to specialise in traditional wooden items once more, in a deliberate attempt to recreate a flavour of the old Timmer Market.

A curious fair was held each May in the ancient Aberdeenshire parish of Christ's Kirk. It was known as Sleepy Market, because it started at sunset and ran throughout the night. Sleepy Market's popularity was entirely due to its unique hours of business. The neighbouring parish of Kennethmont absorbed the parish of Christ's Kirk in the early seventeenth century and continued to hold the fair for about another hundred years. As Rev Mr George Donaldson reported in the *Statistical Account of Scotland*, 1791-1799, it was a change to daytime trading that brought about its demise:

> The proprietor of Rannes has a title to two annual fairs, one at Kirkhill in October for cattle, timber, and merchant goods, and the other at Christ's Kirk in the month of May. This fair was kept on the Green and in the night; hence it was by the people called Sleepy-market. About 35 or 36 years ago, the proprietor changed it from night to day; but so strong was the prepossession of the people in favour of the old custom, that rather than comply with the alteration, they chose to neglect it altogether.

The Rev Mr Donaldson went on to support, albeit somewhat cautiously, the notion that the site on which Sleepy Market took place was the setting of the celebrated ballad, *Christ's Kirk on the Green*, attributed to James I:

> *Was never in Scotland heard nor seen*
> *Such dancing nor deray,*
> *Neither at Falkland on the green*
> *Or Peeblis at the Play*
> *As was-of wowarls as I ween*
> *At Christ's Kirk on a day.*

This claim was reiterated in the *New Statistical Account of Scotland*, 1845.

Until 1707, the goods at Scotland's markets and fairs were sold in units of weight and measurement that were unique to Scotland. An early group of four burghs, Berwick, Roxburgh, Stirling and Edinburgh, jointly established standards for weights and measures to which other burghs generally adhered. In 1369, the burghs of Lanark and Linlithgow took over from Berwick and Roxburgh. Each burgh had its own responsibilities. Edinburgh became the guardian of the standard linear measurement; Linlithgow had responsibility for dry measure and Stirling for liquid measure. Lanark was responsible for a set of national weights that were

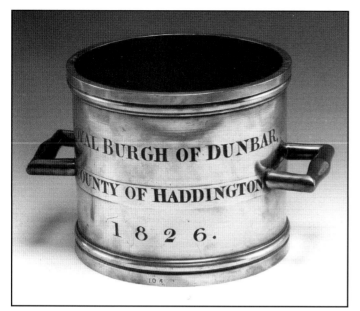

One gallon

made originally from stone and later from brass or lead. Each burgh was required to maintain a physical copy of the various units of measurement so that burgh officers could make sure that traders were not dealing in short measure. Other burghs would buy their own copies from the four custodian burghs.

The standard unit of linear measurement was an ell, a length of 37 inches. Liquid was measured in gallons and pints and the Scots pint of the time was the equivalent of three English pints. Pints were further broken down into choppins, mutchkins and jowcatts. A jowcatt represented a quarter of a mutchkin, a mutchkin was half of a choppin and a choppin measured half of a pint. Weight was measured in stones, pounds and ounces. Decimalisation was still far, far in the future. Traditionally, and somewhat confusingly, dry goods, such as flour and barley, were measured by volume rather than by weight. They were sold in units of pecks, firlots and bolls and there were four pecks to a firlot and four firlots to a boll. After the Union of 1707 and the adoption of uniformity of measure as well as of coinage, the four custodian burghs retained certain privileges and were given the right to supply copies of the new standard measures to the other burghs.

Even when a pedlar attempted to trade quite openly and legitimately, he was most unlikely to be allocated, or even to be able to afford, a prime position at a market or fair. The life of a pedlar has never been a soft option. In medieval Scotland, this peripatetic lifestyle was extremely demanding, both physically and mentally. Many pedlars travelled the country with their goods strapped to their backs and the sheer effort of travelling over rough country weighed down like this must have been enormous. Even at the beginning of the nineteenth century, as Dorothy Wordsworth observed, this was still a hard way to earn a living:

> An old man with a huge hamper of chickens is going to Greenock - a perfect tramper grown over with hair, his clothes hang loosely about him. I heard him say that he had walked twenty miles this morning with that burthen before he took a boat at Tarbert. The men are greatly amused with his stories - he is all fun and rags. It is his business to travel from

2lb weight

house to house in the Highlands, picking up fowls and eggs and any other marketable commodities. An old woman near him, whose store is but a small basket of eggs, inquires of him how they are selling, and his reply makes her look grave.

However, there was, as always, another side to the coin. For a relatively small outlay, a pedlar could set himself up in business; he was free to travel and to manage his own work routine. There was also the possibility of a little tax evasion. To the justifiable annoyance of local merchants, if a pedlar conducted his business speedily, he could sometimes manage to get well away before burgh officials had the chance to get any sales taxes from him.

Pedlars were liable to be met with suspicion wherever they went. A pedlar, unless or until he had established a regular trading route, was necessarily a stranger and was usually assumed to be guilty until proven innocent. There were times when such suspicion was fully justified and not just with regard to sharp practice. In 1604, as yet another outbreak of plague was sweeping across the country, two pedlars sought entry to the town of Ayr. They had with them 'proof' that they were free from disease. They came up against the minister of Ayr, John Welsh, son-in-law of the great John Knox. He was unconvinced by the pedlars' story and urged that they be refused entry, on the grounds that they were certain carriers of disease. The pedlars were forced to travel on to the village of Cumnock where, sadly, the plague spread like wildfire and there was great loss of life.

For some pedlars, like Godric of Finchale, the lifestyle was simply a means to an end. Alexander Wilson financed his literary endeavours with profits from peddling. Wilson was born in Paisley in 1766 and as a young man he became an apprentice weaver. When his apprenticeship was over, he took to the open road and, while he was working as a pedlar, he began to write poetry. He wrote many poems, mostly on the themes of family and working life and, in 1790, he managed to get his collected works published. Unfortunately, he did not set the literary world alight. Four years later he went off to America as an emigrant. Once there, he worked variously as a labourer, a printer and a weaver, before settling on a career as a schoolteacher. At the very beginning of the nineteenth century, Wilson made the acquaintance of an eminent American naturalist, William Bartram, who introduced him to the study of ornithology. This became his passion and Alexander Wilson finally found something that absorbed him totally and to which he could become fully committed. He travelled extensively and began a series of detailed drawings of American bird life. These drawings were the basis of a massive nine-volume work, *American Ornithology*. Once the first volume had been published, the complete nine-volume set was made available on subscription for an amazing $120. The project depended on the sale of two hundred and fifty subscriptions. Andrew Wilson himself, doubtless drawing on the skills that he had learned as a pedlar in Scotland, succeeded in finding a full complement.

Andrew Wilson's career path was unusual in that he was an emigrant who was a pedlar not in his adopted country, but in his native land. It is more usual for someone to work as a pedlar when they arrive in a new country, rather than before they leave the old one. Nineteenth and early twentieth century immigrants to Britain often turned to peddling as a short term expedient, until they had earned enough money to establish themselves in a more settled line of business. One of the many to conform to this pattern was Reo Stakis, who came to Scotland from Cyprus in 1927. When he arrived, he had just £60 in cash and a suitcase full of Lefkara lace. He sold this lace work door to door and it proved extremely popular in the affluent suburbs of Glasgow. Reo Stakis used the proceeds from this successful enterprise to fund his first restaurant. He went on to build a vast hotel empire.

There was an inexorable decline in traditional peddling as more and more people moved from the countryside to the towns and cities. It persisted for longer in rural areas than in the towns and cities and it is possible that in the remoter parts of Scotland it has not entirely died away. In his account of life on Colonsay in the late 1960s, John McPhee wrote about an elderly pedlar who still visited the island several times a year, making his rounds with his goods strapped to his bicycle.

There are still markets in Scotland too and not all of them have a tradition stretching back to medieval times. Maggie McIvor founded Glasgow's notorious 'Barras' in the 1920s. Maggie's connection with markets began when she was only twelve, when she looked after a fruit barrow that belonged to her mother's friend. She moved from this Parkhead stall to open her own fruit shop in Bridgeton and it was while she was on a buying trip at the fruit market that she met her future husband, James McIver. James and Maggie McIver went into business together, renting horses and carts to street traders who could not afford their own and, as soon as they could afford it, they bought a piece of land in the Calton district of Glasgow. For some years previously, a street market had been held on Clyde Street in the city centre, but in the early twenties it was closed down. Maggie McIver quickly stepped in. She offered to rent out pitches on her land and was soon running a market that had a complement of more than three hundred barrows. From the very beginning, the market was renowned for its rumbustious atmosphere and stallholders' patter; however, many of its traders dealt in second-hand clothes and the relentless Glasgow rain did little to improve the appearance of their stock. Maggie, enterprising as ever, came up with an idea that would protect both their stock and her thriving business. In 1929, she had part of the site transformed into a covered market and, although the remainder of the site was still available for open-air selling, the second-hand clothes dealers were able to move indoors, where they were protected from the inclement weather.

Maggie developed her market site again in 1934. Dance halls had become extremely popular in the thirties and nowhere more so than in Glasgow. The ever-shrewd Maggie McIvor realised that she could add a second storey to her market building and open it to the public as the Barrowland dance hall. It was a runaway success. The high-spirited atmosphere of the market set the tone for the dance hall and the two ran happily in tandem for many years, until a fire gutted the famous ballroom in 1958. The ballroom was reinstated, but the popularity of dance halls was on the wane and it was soon used primarily as a location for pop concerts. Latterly, the market has also undergone some transformation. The Barrows Enterprise Trust was formed in 1982 to restructure and rejuvenate the market and its surrounding area. Today, the Barras still makes a lively and colourful contribution to the life of Glasgow's East End.

The Grassmarket and Edinburgh Castle

Chapter 3

An enlightened age

By the mid-seventeenth century, things were beginning to change. The first fixed shops had opened in the towns and, very gradually, the absolute primacy of the markets and fairs began to slip. The first fixed shops were not really shops as we know them today. Some traders ran their businesses from the ground floor area of their homes; others operated from booths or stalls. The first wooden 'buithes' in Edinburgh were built facing the Church of St Giles in the mid-fifteenth century. There is a record of a locksmith working in Edinburgh in 1586 and, as the trade became more widespread and stallholders were able to make their booths secure, they were renamed the Luckenbooths, 'lucken' meaning locked. Many of them were home to the bookbinders, who sold and sometimes published books as well. Bookselling has a long history in Scotland. Some very early books had been available at Scotland's markets and fairs, but the trade began to develop properly in the late sixteenth century. Bookselling was centred on Edinburgh but it spread quickly to other towns. The first recorded date for a bookseller in Perth was 1587, for Glasgow and St Andrews it was 1599 and for Aberdeen, 1613. Literacy levels in Scotland were relatively high. By the 1690s, approximately nine out of ten parishes in the Lowlands and in the southern and eastern Highlands had provision for basic schooling. The Scottish Education Act of 1696 stated that a school should be established in every parish in the country. Sir John Sinclair, in his *Analysis of the Statistical Account of Scotland*, 1826, wrote that 'in former times, the commons of Scotland were considered to be the most enlightened people of that rank in Europe'.

There was a ready market in Scotland for reading material at all levels, from the weightiest of academic tomes to the most sensational of 'penny dreadfuls'.

Allan Ramsay, Edinburgh wig-maker, bookseller and poet, started the first circulating library in Britain in 1726. His library and bookshop premises were at the east end of the Luckenbooths. He had a booth that had previously been occupied by the London Coffee House. Some of the more self-righteous citizens of Edinburgh promptly accused him of supplying villainous, profane and obscene material to his customers. One can only assume that they could afford to buy their own reading material. Everyone else must have thought that it was a wonderful idea. Indeed, circulating libraries soon sprang up all over the country.

Mercat Cross and Luckenbooths, c. 1752

Allan Ramsay was born in Lanarkshire in about 1685 and, as a young man, was apprenticed to an Edinburgh wig-maker. He became a burgess in 1710 and opened a shop in the Grassmarket. Ramsay was not just a wig-maker. He was also a talented poet and he relished the literary life. His issued his first poems as broadside sheets. They sold for a penny and proved extremely popular. He soon lost what little interest he had ever had in wig-making and gave it up in 1720 to become a bookseller. Like most booksellers of his day, Ramsay dabbled in publishing. He had a great deal of success publishing his own poetry, most notably his pastoral verse drama, *The Gentle Shepherd*, to which he later added songs. He had a particular interest in early Scots poetry and wrote a number of additional verses to the *Christ's Kirk* poem ascribed variously to James I and James V.

Ramsay's career was not all plain sailing. He had a keen interest in the theatre and opened a playhouse in Carubber's Close. Unfortunately he lost a lot of money on the venture because the Town Council soon closed it down. Allan Ramsay was a man of some style. He had an octagonal house built at Castlehill, near the top of the Royal Mile. He called his house the 'Goose-pie', because this was what it most closely resembled. Allan Ramsay died in January 1758. He was buried in Greyfriars' churchyard and there is a rather striking marble statue of him, resplendent in his silk nightcap, at the junction of Princes Street and the Mound.

In the eighteenth and nineteenth centuries, pedlars, known as chapmen or packmen, travelled the country selling printed pamphlets, news broadsheets and booklets that were known as chapbooks. These

were often shoddily produced and poorly illustrated. They were usually badly printed on poor quality paper, but they were cheap and they became extremely popular. They satisfied a growing demand for affordable mass-market reading. Many of the chapbooks, such as *The Dying Groans of John Barleycorn*, *The Young Creelman's Courtship to a Creelwife's Daughter, 2 Parts* and *Black Eyed Susan and the Sailor's Lamentation*, were deliberately given titles that would entice the reader to buy. However, they were not all light hearted. The more serious reader was also catered for, with poetry, political argument and religious tracts. Many of the chapbooks were produced for children. These were the first children's books and most often comprised retellings of folk tales, such as *The History of Robin Hood* or fairy stories. Some were easy-reading versions of books that had been written for adults. The content of the chapbooks was often illegally 'borrowed' from

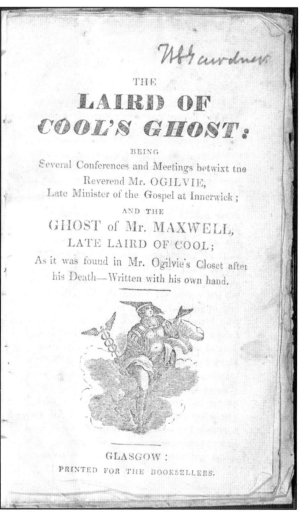

The title page of a popular chapbook, The Laird of Cool's Ghost, *published in 1799*

other sources. Many were crude abridgements of previously published works. Allan Ramsay complained long and hard about a chapbook printer who 'spoil'd my sense, and staw my cash'. There were sufficient numbers of chapmen for them to form their own guild and, until the late nineteenth century, the Guild of Chapmen gathered at Prestonpans each year, to elect their 'king'.

John Smith Son (Glasg Ltd, 57 St Vinc Street, Jan 1998

From 1773 until his death in 1815, William Creech, sometime bookseller to Robert Burns, conducted his bookshop and publishing business from the same Luckenbooth base that Allan Ramsay had once used. Under Creech's tenancy, it became the favourite meeting place of Edinburgh's literary set. William Creech was fortunate in his friends. His mother's close friendship with the wife of Alexander Kincaid, His Majesty's Printer for Scotland, brought him an early partnership in Kincaid's business and, when Kincaid opted to give all of his time to printing, Creech was left the sole owner of the bookselling and publishing arm of the business. His own long-term friendship with Lord Kilmaurs, the son of the Earl of Glencairn, brought him an introduction to Robert Burns and a lucrative association with the poet. Creech was a prominent citizen of Edinburgh. He became a member of the Town Council in 1780 and a magistrate in 1788 and, in that same year, Creech served on the jury at the trial of the infamous Deacon Brodie. He went on to write and publish an account of the trial. William Creech was appointed Lord Provost of Edinburgh in 1811.

Creech was famous for having a 'careful' streak. Although he frequently entertained the glittering literati of his day, he was known to offer them little in the way of refreshment and when he set up his deal with Burns, his terms were canny. In 1787, it was agreed between them that Creech would become Burns' agent and sell a second edition of Burns' poems on subscription. Creech agreed to pay Burns 100 guineas up front, plus the subscription money. In return, Burns assigned his copyright in the poems to Creech. This agreement left Creech free to publish Burns' poetry thereafter without paying him another penny.

Creech bought many of the subscription copies to sell in his own shop. He bought them for five shillings and sold them for six. There was no shortage of takers. Although Burns was reasonably satisfied with the deal that he had struck with Creech, it was not without its aggravations. William Creech's parsimony was legendary. He turned late payment into an art form and many increasingly irascible letters were exchanged before Burns received any money from him at all.

As a result of his irritation with Creech, Burns was pleasantly surprised by the Glasgow bookseller, John Smith. Shortly after his meeting with Smith in 1788, Burns wrote to him, saying 'You seem a very decent sort o' folk, you Glasgow booksellers; but eh! they're sair birkies in Edinburgh.' Smith took up a subscription for a dozen copies of the second edition. He was then appointed distributing agent for all Glasgow subscriptions and agreed to take a modest fee of just 5% for the task.

John Smith & Son is Scotland's oldest independent book retailer and lays claim to being the oldest continuously trading bookseller in the world. The first John Smith, the company's founder, was the youngest son of the Laird of Craigend. He went first into the army, but was wounded in Flanders in 1747 while fighting the French. Smith returned to Glasgow and opened his first shop in 1751. This shop was in the Trongate, opposite the Old Wynd. In his first years of trading, John Smith sold tobacco, snuff, tea, coffee and stationery, as well as books, and in the third year of his business, he opened a circulating library. This was the first such library in Glasgow. Ten years later he moved to new premises and placed the following entry in the *Glasgow Journal* of Thursday 16th June 1763:

> John Smith, Bookseller Glasgow, has removed his circulating library from the head of the New Street, to a commodious shop in Mr Donaldson's land in Trongate, opposite the Tron church, where he continues his circulating library as formerly and at the usual terms, viz. ten shillings per year, five shillings and sixpence per half year, three shillings per quarter, one shilling and sixpence per month and one penny per night, catalogues consisting of near 1500 volumes to be had at the library, price four pence, every new performance on amusing or instructive subjects will be added to the library immediately upon its publication.

The 'commodious' premises of which John Smith was so proud actually measured just sixteen by fourteen feet! The first John Smith retired at fifty-seven, although he lived until he was well into his nineties, by which time his grandson, the third of that name, had been in the business for a considerable time. When the last John Smith died in 1849, so did the family's involvement in the firm.

The business continued to prosper under new management and became a limited company in 1909. In the early years of the twentieth century, a branch of John Smith was opened in very close proximity to the University of Glasgow. This was the first of many university bookshops opened by the company. This venture laid the foundation for the path that the company has followed since the closure in 2001 of its flagship store in Glasgow city centre's St Vincent Street. Of the ten shops that John Smith & Son has in Scotland today, eight are on university campuses.

Almost from its very beginning, the Scottish book trade had not been confined to the major cities, although provincial booksellers were rather less likely to be specialist booksellers. Patrick Wilson, admitted as a burgess of Brechin in 1755, was a bookseller who dealt in an incredibly varied range of other goods, as well as books. He sold toys, stationery, wallpaper, glassware, ironmongery and drugs. The *Statistical Account of Scotland*, 1791-1799 said of Brechin:

> One thing however must be noticed, that there is a greater number of shop-keepers in Brechin at present than was ever known at any former period, owing to the great increase of people, which occasions a greater demand for shop commodities.

Patrick Wilson's diversification is an indication that one trader at least was willing and eager to plug the gaps in Brechin's provision.

As a bookseller, Wilson is known to have purchased books from a variety of sources, including John Fairbairn in Edinburgh and John Duncan in Glasgow. He bought a wide variety of chapbooks, numerous Bibles, and titles such as *The Gentle Shepherd, Farquhar's Sermons, Buchan's Domestic Medicine* and *Ramsay's Gazetteer*. He also sold copies of a work that had particular local interest, *A Description of the County of Angus*, published in Dundee in 1793.

Bookselling in Edinburgh meanwhile was growing apace and the trade was not all strictly legitimate. Allan Ramsay was far from being the only person to have liberties taken with his work. There was a huge trade in copyright evasion. James M'Cleish of South Frederick Street in Edinburgh, 'bookbinder, bookseller, circulating library and publisher', was just one of many who thought it worth the risk to sell pirated editions. William Johnston of London sued him in 1773, for selling a pirated edition of Henry Brooke's *Fool of Quality*. Presumably M'Cleish was unabashed and undaunted. He faced further prosecutions in 1774, for selling a pirated edition of Chesterfield's *Letters*, and in 1775, for selling a pirated edition of the works of Sterne.

James Thin, on the other hand, was a righteous and upstanding gentleman. He was an elder of the church and had once thought seriously of a career in the ministry. He had a lifelong passion for hymnology and amassed a collection of some 2,500 hymnbooks. James Thin founded the family firm that went on to become more or less the Edinburgh equivalent of Glasgow's John Smith & Son. He began his apprenticeship at the age of eleven in 1836 and later recalled that, although at that time the population of Edinburgh was only about 136,000, the number of booksellers in the city was as high as 105. Probably twelve of these were really only stationers, but the proportion still seems astonishingly high. The city of Edinburgh had more bookshops per head of population than any other city in Great Britain. By the time that James Thin wrote his autobiographical memoir in 1905, although the city's population had almost trebled, the number of booksellers had not increased at anything like the same rate and it stood at 134.

In 1848, James Thin went into business on his own account and opened a small shop at 14 Infirmary Street. This now forms part of the stationery department of the present day South Bridge shop. The 1840s were a momentous literary decade and there could hardly have been a better time to go into bookselling. The Bronte sisters,

James Thin, South Bridge, Edinburgh, with James Thin standing in doorway, c1900

Dickens, Thackeray, Elizabeth Gaskell and Disraeli were all writing at this time, as were Macaulay, Carlyle and John Stuart Mill. Anthony Trollope and George Eliot were lurking in the wings. In 1853, James Thin was doing so well that he was able to expand and he leased the two rooms above his shop. However, to reach the entrance to these rooms he had to go around the corner and it was impossible to communicate between the two sets of premises without using a speaking tube. This inconvenience was short lived however, as two years later he acquired a lease on 55 South Bridge and he was able to knock through and connect his two buildings. The next advertisement that he placed was as, 'The largest retail bookselling establishment in Edinburgh'.

The company founded by James Thin developed and adapted over very many years. Branches of James Thin were opened in other parts of Scotland and other parts of Edinburgh. Like John Smith & Son, the company moved into academic bookselling and established bases at Heriot-

Bookselling in Glasgow, 2002

Watt and St Andrews universities. Most unusually for a retailing company with so long a history, James Thin remained a family firm throughout its 150 years. Many of the original James Thin's descendants worked in the business and they always comprised the majority of the company's board. In 1994, the company ventured south of the Border and bought twenty bookshops in England, doubling its size in one fell swoop. However, this expansion proved to be a step too far and it is thought to have been a major contributory factor in the ultimate failure of the business in January 2002.

Latterly, it has become extremely difficult, almost impossible, for independent booksellers to compete against the giant multinational bookselling chains that dominate in Scotland's shopping malls and city centres. To have any real chance of success as an independent, a bookshop has to offer something that is unique. Clarissa Dickson Wright opened her Cooks Book Shop in Edinburgh in 1995. She has a high media profile as a newspaper journalist and as one of television's 'Fat Ladies'. Such publicity has done her business no harm at all. Her encyclopaedic knowledge of her subject has helped just as much; she gleefully relates that she has even managed to trace a book for a customer who could tell her nothing more than that her grandmother once owned a copy and that the volume was pink! She makes it a point of honour to try to match the book to the customer, acknowledging that it is of little benefit to her business to sell a beginner a cookery book that demands advanced cooking skills. Such a service is not confined merely to those who visit the shop, but is offered by fax and e-mail too. Clarissa Dickson Wright invites customers to send her what few details they might have of cookery books that they are trying to trace and says that even size or colour can often be enough. Hopefully, whatever else is lost, there will always be a place for a niche bookseller with specialist knowledge and a stock to match.

Chapter 4

"A nation of shopkeepers"

C hanging patterns of employment meant that for the majority of the population self-sufficiency had become a thing of the past: obviously, self-sufficiency was not a viable option in the towns and, as people in towns and in the countryside became more prosperous generally, everyone wanted ready access to consumer goods. It was gradually becoming easier to move goods around the country. The road system in Scotland had been truly appalling. At the beginning of the nineteenth century, it could take as long as two weeks to transport goods from Selkirk to Edinburgh, a distance of only thirty-eight miles, and even the road between Glasgow and Edinburgh was so rough and in such poor condition that it was impassable in many places during the winter. A network of Turnpike Trusts had been established to address the dreadful road conditions. These trusts were empowered to charge tolls for travel on roads within their jurisdiction and this revenue was intended for road maintenance and improvement. As the roads were improved, it became easier for carts and wagons to be used all year round and greater quantities of goods could be transported from place to place at any one time. At the same time, the development of the railway system and, to a lesser extent, the canals provided welcome new haulage options.

Mid-seventeenth century records for a fairly typical small town, the Royal Burgh of Dumfries, show that thirty-two merchants were running permanent businesses from booths and that even more were thought to have been operating from their homes. Their stock was entirely geared to

Looking towards the village of Lairg

the needs of the rural community in and around Dumfries. Most of these merchants ran general stores, with stock that ranged from cloth, haberdashery, salt, grain and ironmongery to writing materials; a few specialised in things like animal skins or linen. Much of their stock would have been displayed outside, to attract the attention of potential customers, because until the invention of cast glass in 1688, glass for display windows was prohibitively expensive. However, once the mass-manufacture of clear, plate glass got underway, shopkeepers could move indoors without handicap. By the early part of the nineteenth century, most towns had a reasonable variety of permanent, fixed shops and most sizeable villages had, at the very least, one general store.

William MacDonald opened a general store in the remote Highland village of Lairg in 1809. In fact, the opening of his shop was really the beginning of Lairg village. Before the shop was opened, there was no actual settlement on the loch side and all the cottages and farmhouses were up on the hills. Mr MacDonald maintained a painstakingly detailed daily record of his business transactions in a ledger that he called his day book. His day book for the years 1811-1818 has survived and it makes fascinating reading. Sheep farming was of crucial importance to the area around Lairg and very many of his customers were shepherds. Others came from a fairly wide spectrum that included a bridge builder, servants, masons, merchants, tailors, millers, weavers, the minister, the schoolmaster and even the laird.

His stock was amazingly comprehensive. He kept hardware, leather goods, haberdashery, material, clothes, dry grocery and a variety of miscellaneous items. Some of his stock was imported from overseas, such as indigo dye from India, sugar and coffee from the West Indies and tobacco from America and Cuba. Of the hardware items, his record shows that a pair of horseshoes was sold for two shillings, six good table knives for four shillings and a spade for five shillings and sixpence. A leather cape cost three shillings and sixpence; a blue bonnet went for two shillings and three pence. A lucky child was bought an ounce of peppermint drops for four pence; his mother needed six pence for an ounce of standard quality tea. A tobacco pipe was a bargain at just one penny, whereas a Bible cost as much as three shillings and sixpence. Not all purchases were made with money alone and sometimes goods and services were taken in part payment. John Murray provided the hire of a horse to Tain in exchange for five shillings and seven pence worth of goods from the shop; Duncan Mackintosh supplied a hide, valued at ten shillings and nine pence. After William MacDonald's death, the village store passed to his son, Donald, and then to his grandson, George. It remained in the hands of the MacDonald family for almost a hundred years.

A corner shop in Argyll

Not all Highland villages were as well served as Lairg and Elizabeth Grant recalled little in the way of shopping near Rothiemurchus. Yet, whilst they had no shop, the Grants of Rothiemurchus were pretty well provided for. Life on their Highland estate was a model of bucolic self-sufficiency:

> At this time in the highlands we were so remote from the markets we had to depend very much on our own produce for most of the necessaries of life. Our flocks and herds supplied us not only with the chief part of our food, but with fleeces to be wove into clothing, blanketing and carpets, horn for spoons, leather to be dressed at home for various purposes, hair

for the masons. Lint seed was grown into sheeting, shirting, sacking, etc...We brewed our own beer, made our own bread, made our own candles; nothing was brought in from afar but wine, groceries and flour, wheat not ripening well so high above the sea. And yet we lived in luxury, game was so plentiful, red deer, roe, hares, grouse, ptarmigan, and partridge; the river provided trout and salmon, the different lakes pike and char; the garden quite abounded in common fruits and common vegetables; cranberries and raspberries overran the country, and the poultry yard was ever well furnished.

MacDonell of Glengarry

Colonel Alasdair Ranaldson MacDonell of Glengarry married Rebecca Forbes, the daughter of an Edinburgh banker, in 1802. He took his young bride away from the bustle of the capital city to his isolated Highland mansion and a way of life similar to that of the Grants of Rothiemurchus. Rebecca's daughter, Louise, gave an account of her mother's adjustment to rural living in a series of memoirs that she wrote for *Blackwood's Magazine* in the 1890s:

On coming to the Highlands she was somewhat bewildered by the sort of life that she had to lead. Instead of going to the shops for butcher-meat, whole animals were brought into the larder at once; and, that she might really understand how to arrange the pieces for use at table, she got a sheep cut up exactly as if it had been a bullock. The smallness of the sirloins and rounds that this produced may be imagined, but she learned her lesson. Soon after she went north the housekeeper said she was short of needles. To my mother's amazement she heard that none could be got nearer than Inverness, forty-two miles distant. The needles being an absolute necessity, a man with a horse and cart had to be sent for them.

In 1822, the Caledonian Canal was opened up and their situation improved.

In the far south of Scotland, the St Boswells village store grew out of a cottage industry. The villagers of St Boswells had to travel the few miles to Selkirk to buy groceries before their first village shop opened in 1839. The St Boswells Fair still took place each July and, once a year, it gave the villagers the opportunity to buy a variety of goods: hardware, household equipment, books and toys. However, this fair was held principally for the sale of livestock and, by the middle of the nineteenth century, its

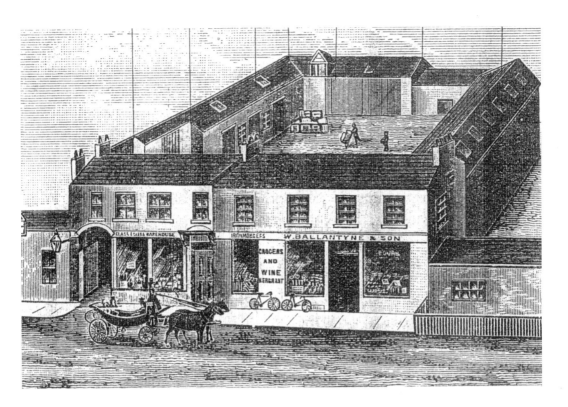

popularity was waning slightly as other livestock markets were opening up in the area. Margaret Ballantyne, the wife of the first Walter Ballantyne, used to make toffee at home to sell to her neighbours. She did sufficiently well with her toffee that she decided to respond to requests from her customers and branch out by stocking a few selected grocery items. Margaret's low-key domestic enterprise laid the foundation for the business, Walter Ballantyne & Sons, Provision Merchants, which operated in St Boswells for almost 140 years, from 1839 until 1978. As the population of St Boswells grew in the 1840s, Ballantyne's business grew with it. After just eight years, the shop moved from its original premises to a building called Fawsley Cottage and, in 1866, they were able to expand still further when they managed to buy the property next door. The land on which Fawsley Cottage once stood was later to become Ballantyne's car park. Like MacDonald's of Lairg, Ballantyne's was an enduring family business. Walter and Margaret Ballantyne survived until the 1890s, but their son, who was also called Walter, took over the running of the shop from 1865. During his tenure, he obtained a liquor licence so that Ballantyne's could sell alcohol. In 1891, he made way for his elder son, yet another Walter. This third Walter was joined in the business by his younger brother, James Kerr, whose sons, Walter and Norman, ran the business together after their uncle's death.

The records that survive for 1909 show just how much the business had developed from the grocery store of 1839. As well as their core stock,

Walter Ballantyne & Sons

Ballantyne's sold kitchen equipment, linoleum, china and glass, stationery, bedsteads and bedding, luggage and toiletries. The shop acted as the local garden centre and sports shop, selling barbed wire and garden seed, golf clubs, curling stones and hockey sticks. It also sold animal feed, guns, gunpowder and petrol. This was one-stop shopping, country-style, very similar to that described by Neil Munro in *The Looker On*:

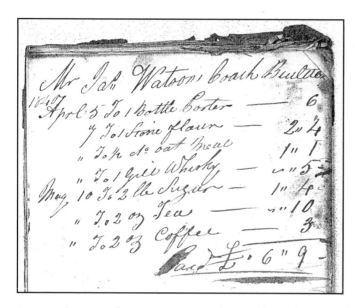

An extract from the detailed memorandum book kept by Borders innkeeper and grocer, James Stoddart, between 1839 and 1841

You could always get oatmeal, tea and sugar, ham, butter, cheese and eggs there; indeed, all the concomitants of any kind of meal; every requisite for housewifery, and even conversation lozenges for moods of love, but a stranger could hardly have guessed that he was in a grocery except for the pile of wooden cheeses with a genuine cheddar on the top. Of every variety of screw-nail there is in nature, MacGillivray had at least a gross. Hinges, locks, door handles, brass bedstead knobs, cutlery and tools, tickets, gimp-pins and sparables, oil cans and coffin-mountings - they were somewhere in the shop if you gave William just a little time to look about for them.

It was generally admitted in the parish that he could not be beaten for boots and braces; his range of oil-cloths and linoleums was extensive; for several years you could not get near the hams because of an American organ he had laid in when a new lady school teacher had started giving music lessons.

Toys! Of course there were toys; every kind of toy you could imagine - sixpenny caoutchouc balls and jumping jacks, dolls, peeries, model boats, mechanical mice, baby's rattles, lead soldiers, squeakers, skipping-ropes, tow-guns and Jack-in-the-boxes…'From a Needle to a Steam Yacht' - an Oban merchant's slogan - was MacGillivray's ideal, slightly modified on account of the limitations of his premises.

It became common practice for the owners of mills, mines and factories to set up general stores in the workplace. In many cases it was not altruism that prompted them to do so: these shops were another source of profit. In general the owners charged very high prices. Nevertheless, workers had little option other than to use them because

Trade token

their long working hours left them little time to go elsewhere. The shortage in the supply of coins presented employers with the opportunity to lock their workers into the system still further. They would often pay the workers' wages, in part at least, with trade tokens that could only be redeemed in the employer-owned store. The Truck Act of 1831 attempted to control this abuse. It prohibited the payment of wages in goods, tokens or anything other than the current coins of the realm. Unfortunately, this legislation was sometimes ignored and applied only to certain specified trades. Its provision was extended in 1887, to cover almost all manual workers.

But not every employer was out to take advantage of his work force when he proffered tokens in lieu of coins. Robert Owen certainly was not; Owen was a model employer. In 1799, he and his partners bought the mill at New Lanark from his father-in-law, David Dale. Owen was a man of very strong convictions. He had no doubt that education was the way to a better society and campaigned for a general reduction in working hours in factories so that the workers had time to continue their education. He adhered passionately to the theory that it is the environment in which a person is brought up and educated that is the determining factor in the

New Lanark village store

formation of character. Owen was no idle theorist; building on the work of his father-in-law, who had himself been a beneficent employer and much concerned with the welfare of his workers, he put his ideas into practice. He opened a village school at New Lanark that provided educational and recreational facilities for the whole community and he opened a village store that offered good and wholesome food at very reasonable prices. Before Owen opened the company store, many of the mill workers were in debt. They had been at the mercy of privately-owned shops that sold goods of inferior quality at exorbitantly high prices.

Owen appreciated just what could be done by economies of scale. He bought from suppliers in bulk and was able to sell for 20% less than the privately-owned shops. He issued 'Tickets for Wages' to his employees that were worth either five shillings or half a crown. These vouchers could be exchanged for goods at the village store and, because the store gave such good value and even though their actual wages were only moderate, the mill workers were more than happy with the arrangement. They could buy household goods, such as cutlery, crockery, cooking utensils, soap and candles, as well as food. The workers could even buy whisky from the store, although any worker who habitually drank to excess could be quite sure that he would face dismissal. Many items on sale were produced locally. The company had a farm at Bankhead, close to the mill, and its own slaughterhouse within the village. There was a seven-acre garden where more vegetables could be grown and, shortly after he left the mill in 1825, his successors carried out Owen's plan to build a bakehouse for the baking of bread.

Edinburgh had long been a shopper's delight. As early as 1792, Robert Heron wrote about the city's shops and the range of goods that they carried in the most approving terms:

> The most considerable branch of its trade is that retail trade which it possesses as the seat of fashion, and the commercial centre of intercourse for Scotland. Hence those splendid shops which line its streets. Hence is it, that many of its richest and most respected citizens are simply shopkeepers. What vast quantities of cottons, of linens, of silks, of woollen stuffs are retailed here. What abundance of liquors and of grocery goods of all kinds. The cabinetmaker earns very large sums. The tailor is amongst the most considerable gainers. The materials for the retail trade are supplied by a very large importation. From the circumjacent country are brought grain, whisky, sheep, beeves, swine, poultry, wildfowl, fish, cheese, butter, milk, eggs and indeed all articles of fresh provisions. From England comes an innumerable variety of articles, partly its raw produce, partly its manufactures and in part imported by the English from Foreign Countries.

Gorebridge Globe Market

Dorothy Wordsworth was equally complimentary about the high standards of the city's fruit shops and their locally grown produce. In *Journal of my Second Tour in Scotland*, 1822, she noted the following:

> At Edinburgh 'Clyde Fruit' is inscribed on the signboards of the choice fruit shops. I have often stopped in Princes Street to admire the tasteful arrangement of pyramids of those apples, the pyramids placed according to their colours, so as to produce the effect of gradation or contrast.

It is unlikely that either of them would have been quite so taken with the Globe Market. The Globe Market was based in Edinburgh, but it became so popular with the inhabitants of the Midlothian village of

Gorebridge that they adopted it as their own. In the late nineteenth century, two Edinburgh food importers, Farquhar and Tarrell, ran a number of shops in various parts of the city. The largest branch was in the city centre in Jeffrey Street. It was called the Globe Market because a large globe light hung over the entrance. This globe became the company's trademark. Farquhar and Tarrell specialised in buying consignments of different types of food that were no longer at the peak of perfection. Knowing that much of what they bought was rapidly approaching the time when it would have to be dumped, the pair could drive a hard bargain. They then had to move quickly and sell their bargains on to the public at knockdown prices. Much of their stock was only too perishable and any 'fresh' food that had not sold by closing time on Saturday was highly unlikely to be saleable when the shops re-opened on Monday. Consequently, they reduced the prices of 'fresh' food every hour on a Saturday evening. A battle of nerves ensued, as customers tried to judge at what price they should buy and how late they could leave it before finally making their purchases.

Musselburgh Globe Market

The Globe Market became incredibly popular with the people of Gorebridge. They would pack the last train out of Edinburgh's Waverley Street Station back to their village on a Saturday night, weighed down with their spoils from the Globe. There were so many Globe customers on board that the ticket collectors started calling this service 'The Globe Train' and Gorebridge's association with the Globe Market became almost official. The arrival of the Globe Train even had a knock-on effect on late-night shopping in Gorebridge itself. John Cunningham, the baker, kept his shop open especially for the hungry and weary passengers. He always had a supply of freshly baked pies ready as the train drew in and his was not the only shop to try to catch their custom. The popularity of the Globe Market with the inhabitants of Gorebridge led Farquhar and Tarrell to open a branch in the village itself in the mid 1890s. However, they did not stay in business in Gorebridge for long and their shop was taken over by Eric Mackay within about five years. Mr Mackay took care to retain the Globe name and trademark light fitting.

Kemp's licensed grocery gave its name to an Edinburgh junction. Charles Arthur Kemp senior left his native Orkney in 1906 for Edinburgh. Two years later he opened his own licensed grocery store in Restalrig, in the east of the city. It was, quite literally, a corner shop. Word soon got around the neighbourhood that this was the place to buy particularly fine-tasting chickens. They were freshly plucked in the shop's backyard. Mr Kemp maintained his Orkney connection and played on it. He sold large Orkney cheeses that customers could cut for themselves and barrels of salted herrings. As the shop became established, people began to call the corner on which it stood 'Kemp's Corner' and it became a well-known Edinburgh landmark. Charles Kemp's son eventually took over the shop from his father. He ran the shop until his retirement in1982, when it passed out of family hands. The Restalrig area of Edinburgh has undergone significant regeneration recently. To mark the completion of the first phase of the Restalrig regeneration plan, a ceremony was held to re-name the junction between Marionville Road and Restalrig Road. Some ninety-three years after Charles Kemp senior opened his corner grocery shop, his son attended the official re-naming ceremony and saw for himself the new name-plates proclaiming this junction 'Kemp's Corner'.

Robert Garden pioneered floating shop services to remote locations. When he left Aberdeen for Orkney in 1873, there were already a number of village stores in operation, but they carried only a limited range of goods and their prices were rather high. Garden decided to try and build a retail business by taking groceries out to the villages on a horse-drawn van. His service proved so popular that he soon built himself a covered wagon and extended the range of goods that he carried. He attracted even more attention when he bought a six-horsepower steam traction engine from the Orkney Road Trustees and used it instead of horses to draw his wagon. Robert Garden was enterprising and ambitious. He went on to open premises in Kirkwall and in some of the outlying villages. He opened his own bakery, lemonade factory and drapery, from which he supplied other shop owners and those who had followed in his footsteps and begun to sell on the road.

He then set his sights on the islands. In 1884 he bought a boat called *Zuna*. He loaded this boat with provisions and sent it off to the South Isles, paving the way for the introduction of regular floating shop services to even the most remote islands. Once his new venture got underway, he ordered a number of purpose-built shop-boats. These boats usually had three sections, one each for grocery, drapery and feeding stuffs and a crew

of at least three, one for each section. More often than not, the crew took goods rather than cash in whole or part payment from the islanders and the lobsters, eggs, dairy produce and knitwear that they brought back were sold on to other customers. Garden used his shop-boats to reach customers in the previously inaccessible areas of north and west Sutherland, before going on to establish permanent bases there too. In 1912, Robert Garden's company was bought out by a Leith company called Tods. Today, Tods of Orkney, as it is now known, markets Stockan & Garden's Scottish oatcakes all over the world.

Orkney floating shop

Other companies followed Garden's example and fitted out boats as general stores and, in the 1930s, floating shops were still operating out of Glasgow, making their way slowly as far as Wester Ross, carrying a huge array of merchandise to tempt their customers, from clocks to clothing, handkerchiefs to hand-lines, manilla rope to Mazawattee tea.

Royal Polytechnic Warehouse

Chapter 5
Department stores and multiples

I n the wake of the Industrial Revolution, more and more people migrated from the countryside to the towns in search of new types of employment. Middle class families began to move out of the city centres to suburbs such as Lenzie on the perimeter of Glasgow that were being built in tandem with the new railway networks. The demand for consumer goods and services was rising steeply and it was a demand that innovative new retailers were only too ready to fill. The middle of the nineteenth century saw the evolution of a new kind of shop, the department store; the latter part of the century saw the evolution of a new kind of retailing, the multiple chains.

John Anderson was one of the groundbreaking entrepreneurs of Victorian Scotland. He was inventive, decisive and flamboyant and a highly gifted businessman. In a profile of John Anderson on 17th December, 1873, *The Bailie* declared:

> John was the never-to be- forgotten discoverer of the elevenpence and three-farthings, which persuade our wives and daughters that they are not spending a shilling.

This simple ploy, of rounding prices down very slightly to make them seem lower than they really were, was highly effective. It was widely copied and is still being used by shopkeepers all over the world.

John Anderson began his career in Perth and moved to Glasgow in 1835. Within eighteen months he was in a position to open his own business. He started on a small scale, with a single-windowed drapery shop in the Gorbals, and worked extremely hard. He was his own salesman, bookkeeper and porter. Whether he was the originator or not, rounding down worked so well for him that he soon needed to move to larger premises in Clyde Terrace. Even this building soon proved too small and he moved his business, now known as the Royal Polytechnic Warehouse, to a prime city centre site in Argyle Street, conveniently near to the bus and tram stops and to the new city centre railway stations, Central, St Enoch's and Queen Street.

In less than eight years, Anderson was employing a workforce of twenty-five salesmen and had set out his stall as a 'universal provider', selling a wide range of goods from toys to patent medicines. Department stores, such as Anderson's were evolving in direct response to the growing middle class market. The Parisian department stores, such as Bon Marché, proved highly influential on the development of such stores in Britain and America. They set stylish standards for magnificent shop fitting and opulent display. Like the Royal Polytechnic, many of the British stores had originally been drapery warehouses, although Harrods in London started as a grocery shop. The Polytechnic was the first 'one-stop' shop in Glasgow and the public loved it. Anderson's Royal Polytechnic Warehouse became so successful that by the time that he celebrated its golden jubilee, the sales force had grown to a complement of over two hundred. He had renamed his store a 'polytechnic' warehouse because, rather oddly, the Clyde Terrace premises had included a lecture hall, a museum and a waxwork display. The review of the Polytechnic in *The Mercantile Age* of December 1882 asserted that it was:

> the only house north of the Tweed where almost everything from the proverbial 'needle to an anchor' is to be found. A mantle, a bonnet, a boot, a needle, a pin, china, hardware, jewellery are all to be had here, and to be had of a superior quality and at astonishingly low prices.

Once he started stocking goods other than drapery, Anderson faced considerable hostility from rival retailers who bitterly resented his encroachment on their territory. In 1849 he alienated the local booksellers when he bought seven tons of publications from the Religious Tract Society. He sold out completely within five weeks. He took on the grocers at the same time and bought six hundred barrels of arrowroot. These were shifted in just two weeks. Anderson had an unerring instinct for guessing what the public would buy and how much they would pay for it. He was never afraid to seize an opportunity and, after the revolution in France in 1848 and the abdication of King Louis-Philippe, Anderson went on buying trips to France to take full advantage of a standstill in French trade. He specialised in buying consignments of remaindered items, all manner of bargain stock from bankruptcy sales and ex-display stock from exhibitions. In 1867, at the Paris Exhibition, he bought so much Austrian merchandise that the Austrian ambassador wanted to give him a medal. The offer was politely declined.

John Anderson had a great flair for merchandising. By the middle of the nineteenth century the Victorian Christmas was gathering momentum and he was very quick to spot the opportunity that this presented. He decorated his store for the Christmas season for the very first time in 1851. With each succeeding year the Polytechnic's Christmas decorations grew more and more extravagant and they certainly brought in the crowds. Anderson was a real showman and in later years he augmented the decorations with magnificent mechanical tableaux. In 1882, thousands of visitors came each day to gaze at the spectacle of the bombardment of Alexandria and the battle of Tel-el-Kebir. Customers had to pay a small charge for this privilege, but the proceeds were distributed to local charities. Anderson then hit upon the novel idea of making a similar charge for entry to the sale that he held each year from 1st-5th January. Customers were asked to pay two pence for admittance. This money too was donated to charitable causes. The charges did nothing to deter the crowds and the charitable donations that the store made were very good publicity. Furthermore, the publicity did not actually cost the company a penny.

John Anderson enjoyed the rewards that his business success brought him. He used some of his new-found wealth to buy a large house in Park Gardens in Glasgow's West End, much to the consternation of his new neighbours. They considered themselves superior and did not relish living cheek by jowl with a purveyor of 'remnants'. They all joined forces and offered to buy him out. They did not know their man. Anderson turned on them. He refused their offer out of hand and threatened that if there was even the slightest hint of a repeat of such nonsense, he would have the front of his house painted 'a lively tartan tint'. Anderson celebrated the golden jubilee of his business in typically exuberant fashion, with a banquet for over six hundred guests at St Andrew's Hall. This was the first large banquet in Glasgow to which women were invited. As well as the usual speeches, guests were entertained by an organ recital during the reception and a musical band during dinner.

John Anderson's two sons succeeded him in business. His Royal Polytechnic Warehouse became a limited liability company in 1900 and was sold to Lewis's for £750,000 in 1929. The store was completely rebuilt by Lewis's to twice its original size. It was to change hands again some sixty years later, when the store underwent yet another major structural transformation, before re-opening in 1991 as part of the Debenham group.

At about the same time that Anderson was starting out in Glasgow, two young men, Charles Jenner and Charles Kennington, were facing an uncertain future in Edinburgh. They had been dismissed from their posts at the drapery store, W&R Spence, for taking time off without permission to go to the Musselburgh Races. Apparently, this setback left them far from downcast and gave them the incentive to embark on their own joint business venture, which they aimed squarely at the New Town carriage trade. They leased business premises in central Edinburgh at 47 Princes Street and were ready to open on 8th May 1838. They placed their emphasis on high quality, high fashion goods and their opening announcement proclaimed:

Jenners, Edinburgh, Scott Monument in foreground

The proprietors have been assiduous in their endeavours to obtain in every instance a quality of goods that will give the most entire satisfaction; and the most energetic means will be constantly used to ensure an uninterrupted supply of novelties.

Business was good and the store underwent a gradual, but steady expansion. By 1860, Jenners had taken over 48 Princes Street and 2-8 South St David Street. By 1875, four new floors were added to the South St David Street frontage and, by 1890, Jenners was the largest retail store in Scotland.

Jenners today is a magnificent store. It owes its present magnificence to a disaster. The original buildings were completely destroyed by a calamitous fire in November 1892. By the turn of the century, it had become very unusual for large stores to offer staff accommodation, but at the time of the fire Jenners had 120 members of staff living on the premises.

Although formally retired, Charles Jenner intervened at once to see that they were all immediately re-housed and compensated for any losses that they had incurred. The business was protected by twenty-three separate insurance policies and arrangements were made for the shop to be rebuilt at maximum speed and in magnificent style. During the intervening period, the shop operated from the Jenners factory site on Rose Street. Charles Jenner died in 1893, over a year before the new store was completed. In his will he left a sum of £8,000 that was to be spent on the decoration of the outside of the building. He stipulated most particularly that female figures should be carved into the decorative columns, as a visible reminder of just how crucial women customers were to the success of Jenners. The new store was officially opened on Wednesday 8th March 1895 and, by two o'clock on the opening day, it had attracted approximately 25,000 visitors. Architecturally, it was based on the Bodleian Library in Oxford and, in the style of the great Parisian department stores, it had gallery floors, grand staircases and an ornate glass roof. As a precaution against fire ever being able to sweep through the length and breadth of the building again, the new shop floor was divided into a series of discrete, connecting areas. Undoubtedly, this was a most successful strategy in terms of safety, but it has not been without pitfall. Unwary new customers find it all too easy to get lost in the labyrinth of the store.

Jenners has become an institution. Long before marketing became a field of academic study, its founders and their successors realised that there was so much more to shopping than buying something. They inculcated a seductive ambience of refinement, taste and quality; they promised service and privilege. Shopping or taking tea at Jenners both confirmed and conferred status. As late as the 1970s, even after the uniformed commissionaires had disappeared, Jenners' customers were spared the hassle and tedium of looking for a parking space. A team of chauffeurs was still on hand to whisk customers' cars away to the garage in Broughton. Unfortunately, this level of service became unsustainable in the late twentieth century and Jenners had to adapt to changing times. The store needed to attract customers from a broader socio-economic spectrum and to become more competitive. Jenners rose to the challenge and has survived where other stores have fallen by the wayside. Although the store has developed and adapted to changing circumstance, its leaders did not altogether lose sight of their original niche market and this is probably what saved it. The old Jenners has not entirely vanished and somehow the store has retained a distinctive aura that sets it apart from its identikit rivals on the high street. Jenners is now the oldest surviving independent department store in the world and is no longer a single site

*Jenners,
Edinburgh,
Fabrics Hall
and Grand
Hall, 1895*

business. The company has outlets at Edinburgh Airport and at the Ocean Drive complex at Leith and further expansion is planned. Ocean Drive is the home of the former Royal Yacht *Britannia* and Jenners sells high quality gifts and souvenirs at its Visitor Centre. The royal connection is a particularly happy one for a firm that was awarded a Royal Warrant by King George V, as long ago as 1911.

Food has always loomed large at Jenners, for customers and staff alike. The heyday of the retaurants was the period from the turn of the century to the outbreak of the Second World War. Generations of Morningside ladies observed the social niceties and gathered over morning coffee or partook of an elaborate and most genteelly served afternoon tea. Customers would travel up from the country to spend the day at the store and enjoy morning coffee, lunch and afternoon tea as part of the service. They could even withdraw to a special lounge and catch up with their correspondence using special Jenners' stationery. Even during the Second World War when rationing was at its strictest, the store provided for the sustenance of its customers. Lunch was served in the store from eleven o'clock and people were prepared to queue a long time for a table. Once a week steak pie was on the lunch menu and omelettes that were made from flaked egg powder became the chef's speciality. Vast quantities of perfectly square-shaped chips were fried each day. The less uniform end pieces of the potatoes were sent off to be used in the staff canteen. Jenners' meringues had long been a firm favourite, but it had been impossible to get hold of enough sugar to keep them on the menu during the war. Then someone hit on the ingenious plan of asking customers who wanted meringues to contribute their own sugar ration. Incredibly, this strategy was taken up and the kitchen staff baked on average some 1,200 meringues each day. However, it proved impossible to save the production of Jenners' handmade chocolates and the speciality ice cream that had been made from thick cream, vanilla essence and French strawberries was also lost.

Before the Second World War, staff at Jenners could opt for a payment package that entitled them to free meals at the store. No restrictions were placed on the quantity of food that an employee could eat. This was an absolute boon to those with a hearty appetite and one particular head cleaner became famous for always taking six boiled eggs for his breakfast. The staff ate roast meat in sufficient quantity to merit the employment of a full-time meat carver, but all roasting and frying for the staff canteen had to be completed by 2.00 pm. This was so that there would be no cooking smells to upset customers who came to have garments fitted in the afternoons. Today, in addition to a Food Hall that stocks all manner of traditional Scottish fare, as well as other more exotic foodstuffs, Jenners has five restaurants. They are all rather less grand and formal than their pre-war counterparts.

Mrs Lizzie Dickson, a cleaner at Jenners, c. 1954

The introduction of the department store changed the face of shopping in Scotland. It was to change still further with the development of multiple retailing. John Menzies was born in Edinburgh in 1808. As a young boy, his father arranged for him to be apprenticed to a local bookseller. He survived a rigorous apprenticeship, working an eighty-four hour week with just a day off on Sunday and New Year's Day and, when it was over, set out for London to try to make his way in the world. Menzies got a job with a bookseller in Fleet Street that placed him at the very hub of bookselling and publishing. On the sudden death of his father in 1833, however, he returned to Edinburgh to look after his stepmother and his sisters. He decided to stay in the city and to open his own shop in Princes Street. His shop appears in *Gray's Edinburgh Directory, 1835* as Bookseller, Stationer and Printseller. John Menzies was a man in a hurry. No sooner had he got his shop off the ground, than he set about establishing a wholesale business. He had made many contacts in the publishing world during his time in London and he soon secured an agency for the London publishing house of Chapman and Hall. He could not have got off to a better start: Chapman and Hall were just publishing *The Posthumous Papers of the Pickwick Club*. As soon as the character of Samuel Weller was introduced in the fifth monthly instalment , the circulation simply leapt and *Pickwick Papers* and its author, a young reporter called Charles Dickens, became publishing and literary phenomena. Menzies' arrangement with Chapman and Hall gave him the wholesaling rights to the novels of Charles Dickens throughout the east of Scotland. This was the proverbial licence to print money and it gave John Menzies' wholesale business an extremely firm foundation. As his business grew, Menzies made many trips to London to renew his acquaintance with former colleagues and to make new contacts. Foremost amongst them was his English alter ego, W H Smith.

In common with most booksellers of the time, John Menzies also did some publishing and had much success with two series in particular: one was a series of Scottish guidebooks; the other was called *Vignette Views*. He also published a sumptuous volume, *Costumes of the Clans*, which retailed for the princely sum of four guineas. Its princely price was matched by its princely dedication. *Costumes of the Clans* was dedicated to the then King of Bavaria, whom the Jacobites regarded as the true heir to the British throne. Menzies' wholesale and retail businesses expanded rapidly. He became the Scottish agent for a new magazine called *Punch* and issued the first edition of what became a regular catalogue for wholesale books.

He also started to sell newspapers, beginning with the *Scotsman*. This was a significant step, because the *Scotsman*, like almost all other newspapers of the time, had only been available previously on subscription from the publisher. Reflecting on the newspaper trade of this time in his memoir, *Reminiscences of Booksellers and Bookselling in Edinburgh in the Time of William IV*, James Thin recalled that there was only one limited exception to this subscription rule and that this was the *Evening Post*. A salesman, who blew a horn to alert potential customers of his arrival, would sell copies of the *Evening Post* in some districts of the New Town. When Menzies began to sell it, the *Scotsman* had a cover price of 7d, of which 4d went to the government in stamp duty. The abolition of duty on newspapers, together with advances in printing and the development of the railway network, contributed to the huge expansion of the newspaper industry in the latter half of the nineteenth century and John Menzies' business more than kept pace.

The introduction of the railway bookstall was crucial to the firm's development. John Menzies was not the originator of the station bookstall; this honour belongs to a man called Horace Marshall, who opened the

Menzies bookstall at Charing Cross Station, North Street, Glasgow

first stall at Fenchurch Street Station in London. W H Smith took up the idea and ran with it in England. He soon dominated the English railway market. John Menzies followed a similar path in Scotland. By 1857, he had acquired the sole rights to operate station bookstalls on all the railway lines in northeast Scotland and on the very first train ferry, on the Granton-Burntisland route. He was initially frustrated in his attempt to win control of the concessions at Edinburgh's two main stations, but he was not a man to give up easily. As well as station bookstalls, Menzies engaged a team of boys to carry tray-loads of newspapers along the platforms at stations where trains did not stop for long enough to give passengers time to get down to buy fresh reading material. The 'basket boys' also plied their wares on the Clyde steamers, before they too were possessed of purpose-built bookstalls.

John Menzies was quick to recognise the other opportunity presented by this burgeoning trade. He set up an agency for newspaper distribution and took full advantage of the head start afforded by his chain of station bookstalls. The basis of a distribution network was already in place. The company took delivery of enormous bales of newspapers from publishers. These were duly separated and delivered to city centre and neighbourhood newsagents, according to their individual requirements. This function, the railway bookstall and wholesale divisions of the John Menzies operation were assuming an ever-greater importance and, in 1859, the company decided to close the original Princes Street bookshop. John Menzies did not re-open on the high street until 1928. A new wholesale warehouse was opened in Hanover Street and within three years Menzies finally won the bookstall concession at Edinburgh Waverley Street Station. In 1868, in a bid to extend his domination of the newspaper distribution trade to the west of Scotland, Menzies opened a warehouse in Glasgow. By the time that John Menzies died in 1879, his business that had begun with a single Princes Street bookshop had grown into a multi-faceted empire. Over a century later, in 1998, the John Menzies company moved out of newspaper retailing altogether. The retailing division of the Menzies group was sold to W H Smith, the business founded by the original John Menzies' English competitor.

By the 1890s, Thomas Lipton had built the largest grocery retailing chain in the world. It had a turnover of in excess of £1 million each year. Lipton was the son of an Irish immigrant couple who ran a small shop in Glasgow's Crown Street, selling Irish bacon, eggs and butter. He was born in Glasgow in 1850. The young Thomas left school at the age of ten and worked hard at a number of different jobs, before setting sail for America at the age of fifteen. Here too, he found it hard to settle in any one job. Eventually, he took up a post with a high-class grocer in New York and his interest was caught. He became totally convinced of the validity of the American approach to retailing. He could see how positively customers responded to the obviously gleaming store. He saw just what could be achieved by eye-catching display and clever advertisement. He learned what he could from his American employer and, in 1869, he returned to Glasgow to put American marketing strategies to work in Scotland. He arrived back in some style. Lipton had saved a not inconsiderable £100 while he was away and he indulged himself by hiring a private carriage to take him on the last part of his journey from the docks to Crown Street. He made sure that nobody would miss his triumphant homecoming. Strapped to the roof of the carriage was a barrel of flour and a rocking chair, brought from America as a present for his beloved mother.

He opened his first shop within two years of his return. It was an 'Irish Market' in the Anderston neighbourhood of Glasgow. His style was distinctive from the outset. The shop was simply fitted, but scrupulously clean and always very brightly lit. Its proprietor was dressed in sparkling white. His aim was to give value for money without compromising on quality. He was prepared to work on far lower profit margins than other grocers and he made a point of paying suppliers without delay, so that he could drive a better bargain. He opted not to offer credit facilities or delivery services to his customers in order to keep his overheads as low as possible. He put his trust in the appeal of keen pricing. He sold ham at half the price of his competitors and butter almost as cheaply. Lipton attracted customers in droves. His opening hours suited his working class customers too. His shop opened at seven in the morning to allow people to buy fresh food for breakfast and did not close until late at night, so that they could shop after they had finished work.

COMING FROM LIPTON   GOING TO LIPTON

The Lipton formula could not fail. Thomas Lipton offered convenience and quality at amazingly low prices. He made sure everyone knew it. As a boy in America, he had seen for himself how advertising boosted sales and was eager to launch his own advertising campaign. As soon as the business got off the ground and he was ready to expand, Lipton commissioned a celebrated cartoonist, Willie Lockhart, to work on a series of advertisements that would be guaranteed to put Lipton's in the public eye and to put the public into Lipton's. Lockhart's cartoons were incredibly effective. An early example shows a woeful-looking line of skinny customers making their way to a Lipton's store. After their visit they are shown marching away briskly, plump, happy and quite rejuvenated, thanks to the magic of Lipton's. The more people laughed at Lipton's cartoons, the more they bought from his stores. By the end of the 1870s, Thomas Lipton was selling 1.5 tons of lump butter, 50 cases of roll butter, 1.5 tons of ham, 1 ton of bacon, half a ton of cheese and 16,000 eggs every day in just four branches in Glasgow. Each shop was in a very carefully chosen location within a working class area. Lipton soon expanded further and opened branches in Paisley, Greenock, Dundee, Aberdeen and Edinburgh. When the Dundee branch opened in 1878, it was on a grand scale. A staff of as many as fifteen salesmen, all smartly

Willie Lockhart's advertisement showing Lipton's satisfied customers

dressed in white uniforms, and three cash boys stood at the ready behind a substantial horseshoe counter. The shop was copiously stocked with hams, bacon, butter and a variety of cheeses.

Spurred on by previous success, Thomas Lipton then took a bold and highly unusual step. He ventured across the Border and began to open stores in England. His first English store was in Leeds and many others soon followed. By 1898, Lipton had built a chain of four hundred grocery stores. As the number of Lipton's branches increased, so did the variety of the foodstuffs that they carried and in the course of the 1890s margarine, jam, mineral water, confectionery, wines and spirits were all introduced.

Thomas Lipton's flair for public relations and advertising was unrivalled. In 1881, he announced that he would bring to Glasgow the greatest cheese in the world and proclaimed that it would take two hundred dairymaids six days to collect the milk from an eight hundred strong herd of American cows to make it. When it arrived, the gargantuan cheese was transported through the streets of Glasgow, drawn by a steam

The Lipton pound note

traction engine all the way from the docks to Lipton's store. It was proudly displayed in the shop window and many came to gawp. Once at the store, they stayed to buy. Lipton capitalised on the cheese's notoriety by studding it with half sovereigns, like a gigantic Christmas pudding, before having it cut and put on sale. Pandemonium ensued as people fought to buy a piece of the cheese and the chance of discovering a half sovereign. The cheese campaign was a masterstroke and Lipton used the basic idea, varying it as necessary, on many occasions and in many different locations. But, of all his advertisements, it was the pound note campaign that attracted most notoriety. Lipton came up with the idea of an advertising flyer that would look like a pound note. The novelty flyer promised that for an expenditure of fifteen shillings at Lipton's on ham, butter and eggs, the customer would actually get food to the value of a pound. Amazingly, his look-alike notes caused a great deal of confusion amongst public and shopkeepers alike. They even resulted in a court case for which Lipton had to pay costs. Nevertheless, he was undeterred. All the publicity that he received was worth far, far more to his business than any costs that he had to pay.

In many countries across the world today, the Lipton name is synonymous not with grocery shops, but with tea. In Japan for instance, a number of department stores have Western-style restaurants that are called

'Lipton's Teahouses'. Lipton's involvement with tea stemmed directly from a desire to keep his costs down. Quite simply, it became more economical for him to grow his own tea than to buy it from someone else. He bought a number of tea plantations in Ceylon and went into production on a grand scale. He sold blended tea in his shops, in brightly coloured packets adorned with photographs of the plantations and the workers, at roughly half the price of his competitors. He also had his own meat packing plant in Chicago, manufactured his own sausages and pies and opened his own curing and jam making facilities. In this way, he was able to control the quality of the goods that he offered in his shops and keep his prices low. Thomas Lipton's great contribution to retailing was to bring good food to working class families at low prices. He set a standard that others were forced to follow. Thomas Lipton was more than a clever businessman. He was also a man of immense personal charm and overcame the barriers to social mobility of his day with rather more ease than John Anderson. A shared enthusiasm for sailing even brought him into the orbit of the King and, incredibly, Edward VII and Thomas Lipton went on to forge a firm, if unlikely, friendship. Lipton even obliged the King by giving a job to George Keppel, the husband of his beloved mistress, that both paid the Keppels well and kept George Keppel away from home.

R·W·FORSYTH·L^{TD}
Boys & Youths Tailors & Outfitters

DRESS HIGHLAND COSTUME   **FULL DRESS COSTUME**

DRESS JACKET AND VEST   DOUBLET AND VEST

Black Cl...   Black Cloth

Velve...   Velveteen or

Super...   Superfine K...

White...   TA...

Scarle...   As illustratio...

Pri...

an...

23

Edinburgh and Glasgow

R·W·FORSYTH·L^{TD}
Boys & Youths Tailors & Outfitters

D.B. REGULATION REEFER
In Government and Worsted Serge and Nap Cloths with Brass Buttons
Price: 14/6 to 30/-

MAN O' WAR SUIT
Essentially a young boy's Suit, correctly made and completely fitted. Regulation Collar, Government Indigo Serge 20/- to 35/-
Extra Trousers to match from 8/6

Edinburgh and Glasgow

R·W·FORSYTH·L^{TD}
Boys & Youths Tailors & Outfitters

"WAVERLEY" SUIT
Knickers with button at knee or Open Shorts, in Scotch Tweeds, also in Navy and Black Serge.
Price: 23/6 to 37/6

D.B. "RUGBY" SUIT
Stylish Model for School or Vacation wear. Fine quality Saxony Tweeds and Navy Serges.
Prices: 23/6 to 35/-

Edinburgh and ...

Chapter 6

A divided society

As the nineteenth century progressed, there was steady growth in all sectors of retailing. In the years between the First and Second World Wars this growth accelerated sharply. There were shops for the rich, shops for the poor and shops for those who were in between; shops where you could buy hunting and fishing equipment, shops where you could buy overalls and shops where you could buy antimacassars. Then, as now, shopping exemplified the divisions in society. Where a person shopped and what they bought was a pretty accurate reflection of their socio-economic status. Equally revealing, was how they paid for this shopping. Middle class customers were the most likely to shop with cash; the wealthy upper classes disdained cash and expected credit. The poor had very little cash and could not get by without credit.

At the upper end of the market, R. W. Forsyth's was elitist to its very core. In about 1930, the firm issued a catalogue of boys' clothing and outfitting that they called 'Men in the Making'. It is a quite remarkable evocation of a bygone age. The introduction assures customers that, 'The boy with a "Forsyth" outfit knows that it is correct - beyond criticism' and concludes:

> In this book we deal with the subject of Boys' Clothing and Outfitting up to the time when he usually emerges from parental control of his wardrobe, to the dignity of selecting his own tailor - when we are still at his service.

Times have certainly changed. Nowadays, parental control of a child's wardrobe is usually lost in toddlerhood. It is difficult to imagine how the young boys of today would respond to the offer of a sailor suit that could be bought in the 'Standard style, correctly designed, Government Indigo Serge' with 'Detachable Collar, Lanyard and Whistle', at prices from twelve shillings and sixpence to twenty-five shillings and sixpence according to size. Forty-five to sixty-five shillings bought a young gentleman about town a black serge and vicuna jacket with a matching waistcoat and a pair of grey hairline trousers and he could rest assured that his cricketing flannels would be tailored from 'thoroughly soap-shrunk' cloth and that his sports shirts could be bought with detachable collars.

Forsyth's was founded in 1872. The original small shop on Renfield Street in Glasgow sold hosiery and gloves. Within a year, the proprietor, the eponymous R. W. Forsyth, had leased two further properties in the same street and begun to sell clothes. His business underwent a rapid expansion and within fifteen years Forsyth's occupied the whole of a remodelled six-storey building on the corner of Renfield Street and Gordon Street. It boasted the very latest in shop fittings. The entire building was 'heated by hot water pipes, and two gas engines of 32 h.p. each provided an electric light installation for illuminating purposes'. In 1907, a branch was opened in Edinburgh, on the corner of Princes Street and St Andrew's Street. Both stores were department stores, but department stores that put particular emphasis on tailoring and the supply of school uniforms and sportswear. There were large tailoring workrooms in both the Edinburgh and Glasgow stores and the firm commissioned goods from outworkers and manufacturers all over Scotland. When the Edinburgh branch opened, Forsyth's became the official robe maker to the Moderator of the General Assembly of the Church of Scotland and supplied academic and ceremonial gowns to the members and dignitaries of various universities and learned societies. They were also the official keepers of the robes of the Order of the Knights of the Thistle.

Forsyth's service to young gentlemen and their parents was not confined to outfitting. Bizarrely, the store also proffered careers counselling. It published a manual of careers for young gentlemen and a few extracts from this were reproduced at the end of their 'Men in the Making' catalogue, just to whet the appetite for more. Their assessment of farming as a career strikes a horribly hollow note today:

> In the home country there are splendid opportunities for the intelligent young man. As Great Britain, since the repeal of the Corn Laws, has become essentially a stock-rearing country, those who wish to obtain the best financial results will undoubtedly go in for the breeding of stock...If the prospects are rosy at home, they are decidedly more so in the Colonies.

There is still a vast amount of prairie land to be fully utilised in Canada; Rhodesia is practically undeveloped; money and ability are in request in New Zealand and Australia.

Co-operative stores were the very opposite of elitist. Their founders were working class men. Robert Owen of New Lanark fame is often credited with being the father of the co-operative movement, but in fact a few small co-operative societies had been established in Scotland even before his ideas became widely known. In about 1769, a group of Fenwick weavers had banded together to establish a co-operative purchasing society and the Govan Victualling Society was formed on Clydeside at the turn of the century. Nevertheless, there is little doubt that the dissemination of Owen's ideas on social justice, together with his work at New Lanark and the New Harmony settlement in America, were hugely influential on the development of the co-operative movement from the middle of the nineteenth century. The Rochdale Pioneers Society was founded in Lancashire in 1844. This was a crucial milestone in the development of the co-operative movement and its eight 'Rochdale Rules' enshrined the philosophy of co-operation and became part of their liturgy. The Rochdale Rules were solemnly read aloud to prospective members at the inauguration of the Barrhead Society in 1866. According to their precepts, the society's profits were to be distributed to each member, in proportion to the purchases that the member had made. The co-op was not always the cheapest place to shop, but the dividend, or 'divi' as it became known, was a great draw. Very often it was the only way in which a family could possibly accumulate any savings. The co-op divi was the salvation of many working class families over the years. Co-operative societies sprang up all over Scotland and, understandably, they were often much resented by the local shopkeepers. They were particularly popular in industrial, mining and weaving areas and it has been estimated that around 130 small societies had been established by 1867 when an umbrella organisation, the Scottish Co-operative Wholesale Society, was established. By 1900, one in every ten Scots was a member and therefore a shareholder of a co-operative society and Scotland was well on its way to becoming 'a nation of shopkeepers' indeed.

The Co-operative Society in West Calder was founded in 1874 by a group of shale miners. They had suffered badly during a protracted strike and wanted to do something that would give them some protection in the future. They opted to divide their union funds amongst the members so that they could be reinvested in a co-operative society. However, when it came to the point, only forty members were actually prepared to subscribe and their joint capital amounted to just £70. Undaunted, a small group was constituted and its leaders began searching for business premises. Eventually they found a double-fronted shop that they leased for a period of two years. Once premises had been secured, the society's president and treasurer set off to Edinburgh to buy stock from a wholesaler. They arranged to have their purchases delivered by rail and the entire committee was present at the station to see their goods arrive. The fledgling society was in business. They were soon in a position to expand and went on to open new branches in places such as Mid Calder, Stoneyburn and Blackburn. In 1895, a new branch was opened at Addiewell of which the society was very proud:

Co-op horse-drawn country delivery van in Jackson Street, Penicuik

> These premises, which consist of grocery and provision, drapery, fleshing, and bakery departments, are conveniently fitted up. The grocery department has a handsome cash office, to which the transactions are conveyed by the modern cash railway from all departments. The drapery department, in which the work of the local post office is conducted, is conveniently arranged to permit of a large business...

Penicuik Co-op tailors' shop, 1899

The Blackburn branch was opened in 1891 with a membership of 100. Its turnover in the first year of trading was £5,360. By the time that the West Calder Co-operative Society held its Jubilee celebrations in 1925, membership of the Blackburn branch had risen to 659 and its sales to £35,000. From the 1870s, the Scottish Co-operative Wholesale Society began to manufacture a lot of its own products. Within about twenty years much of the manufacturing was concentrated on a sixteen-acre site at Shieldhall in Glasgow. By 1913, the co-operative had an annual turnover of £8.97 million in Scotland and membership stood at almost half a million.

Not all societies stood the test of time. The City of Dundee Co-operative Society Ltd was formed in 1897 and it opened more than a dozen shops and its own bakery before the outbreak of war in 1914. This particular society exemplified the co-operative ideal. It fostered a spirit of community, with a choir, children's outings, women's guilds, its own newspaper and a variety of education programmes. However, it became obvious by 1922 that all was not well financially. This was probably down to mismanagement, but the 1920s were difficult years for most businesses. Despite help from the Scottish Co-operative Wholesale Society, the City of Dundee Co-operative was unable to survive. Their business and stock were taken over by the Dundee Eastern Co-operative in 1925.

In time, the co-op went beyond retailing and manufacturing and began to offer services to its members: members could bank with the co-op, book their holidays at co-op travel agencies and be buried by co-op undertakers. The Broxburn Society advertised its banking facilities in 1913, offering to take deposits of as little as one penny and as much as ten shillings at their banking office or any of their shops; in return, they would give $3^3/_4$% interest on immediate withdrawal accounts. The Scottish Co-operative Wholesale Society suffered some difficulty with its banking service in 1973 and merged with its English counterpart. This merger heralded a major reorganisation of the co-operative businesses that culminated in the amalgamation of the retail and wholesale companies in 2000. At the beginning of 2001, the amalgamated company changed its name to the Co-operative Group (CWS) Ltd.

For as long as shopkeepers have had something to sell, they have needed to persuade others to buy. The earliest shopkeepers painted brightly coloured shop signs to attract new customers. In her journal for 1803, Dorothy Wordsworth remarked that the brightly painted shop signs that she saw in the town of Annan made her think of France and Germany:

> the shopkeepers express their calling by some device or painting; breadmakers have biscuits, loaves, cakes, painted on their window-shutters; blacksmiths horses' shoes, iron tools, etc. etc.; and so on through all the trades.

As printing techniques improved, retailers were able to use wall posters and flyers to advertise their wares. There was a huge leap forward in the nineteenth century in direct relation to the rampant growth in newspaper circulation. Advertising in newspapers and magazines proliferated. Just before the First World War, Cole Porter wrote a song that he called *It pays to advertise*. He was far from being the first person to come to this conclusion. By the early years of the twentieth century, 80-100,000 people were working in the advertising industry. A great deal of the advertising output of the early twentieth century was surprisingly sophisticated and sharply targeted. The content of an advertisement, the style of the language and the illustration were all carefully chosen to reflect the taste and lifestyle of the potential customer.

The message delivered by most advertisements was so blatant, that they did everything but say that the particular shop or a product was for

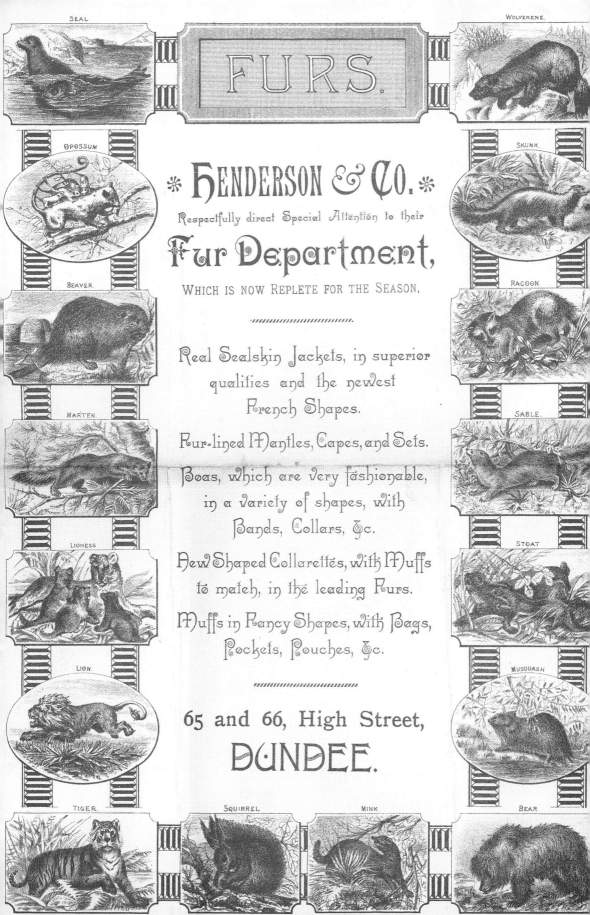

SEAL

WOLVERENE.

FURS.

OPOSSUM

SKUNK.

BEAVER.

RACOON.

MARTEN.

SABLE.

LIONESS

STOAT

LION.

MUSQUASH

TIGER.

SQUIRREL

MINK

BEAR

C.1.16. COPYRIGHT

G. FALKNER & SONS. MANCHESTER.

ENT^R STA HALL

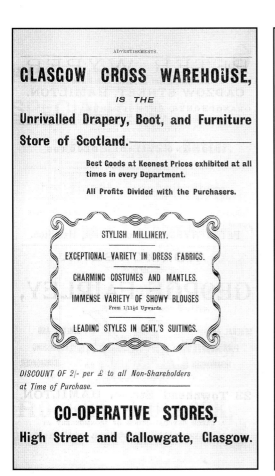

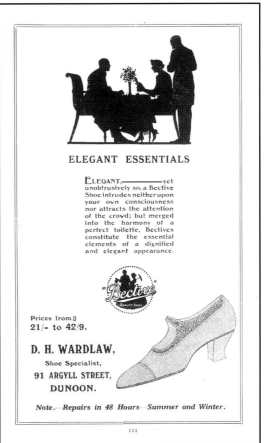

working class, middle class or upper class shoppers only. An advertisement for the Glasgow High Street and Gallowgate Co-operative stores in 1908 featured 'charming costumes and mantles' and an 'immense variety of showy blouses, from one shilling and eleven pence halfpenny upward'. The very idea of 'showy blouses', appealing as it might have been in the East End of Glasgow, must surely have been an anathema to the refined sensibilities of the middle class matrons of Glasgow's West End. Far more to their taste would have been the shoes sold by D. H. Wardlaw of Dunoon:

> Elegant, - yet unobtrusively so, a Bective Shoe intrudes neither upon your own consciousness nor attracts the attention of the crowd; but merged into the harmony of a perfect toilette, Bectives constitute the essential elements of a dignified and elegant appearance.

Everything about this advertisement reinforces the message and the elegantly shod couple, pictured placing their order in a restaurant, are only shown in discreet silhouette. James Cinnamond, Wholesale Cash Clothier and Outfitter of Hamilton, was no subscriber to this 'less is more' philosophy and he was aiming at a different market altogether. His 1908 advertisement is written entirely in cod Scots and peppered liberally with prices and exclamation marks:

AN' NOO, MA FREENS,
YE MAUN KEN THAT
THIS CLAES BIZZNESS!!!
IS YER AIN BIZZNESS!!!
AN' IS KERRIED ON FER YER AIN SEL'S
AN' THE CALLANT'S BENEFIT.

McEwen's of Perth ran an advertisement in the January 1922 edition of *Country Life* that was headed 'Gowns for the South and the Riviera'. Ostensibly, it presupposed that McEwen's customers were just the sorts of people who would go to London for the 'Season' and then travel on to the South of France for a summer holiday. Some of their customers probably did follow this sort of annual routine, but the suggestion that it was the norm must have appealed hugely to those other customers who did not, but who aspired to. From the turn of the century, McEwen's had carried a range of model gowns from Paris that were exclusive to them and could not be bought anywhere else in Scotland.

Mc Ewen's was founded in 1868 when Alexander Walton and James McEwen took over the tenancy of a small drapery store in St John Street in Perth. There were already another fifteen such shops in St John Street and their long-term survival must surely have been open to question. Alexander Walton left the partnership after five years, and, under James McEwen's sole ownership, the business prospered. He built up a successful tailoring service that soon employed a staff of fifty. James McEwen's brother joined him in the business and, in the 1880s, they took on another two managers, Robert Brough and John Miller. Mr Miller was responsible for coats and Mr Brough took charge of the dress material department. Robert Brough made a substantial contribution to the firm and he was rewarded with a partnership in the late 1880s. He was responsible for a change in direction that has guaranteed McEwen's enduring success. He had embarked on a bold new strategy and travelled to France to buy from the great Parisian couturiers. McEwen's soon acquired a national reputation for ladies' fashion and 'Modes from Paris' became their absolute speciality.

The basic designs that Brough brought back from Paris could be copied and adapted in McEwen's workroom. Their standards were extremely high and the quality of their output was such that two Fife

Telegrams: "M'Ewen, Perth."   Telephone : No. 761.

GOWNS for the South and the Riviera

PARIS MODEL GOWNS for *Evening* and *Dinner Wear* in Persian and French Brocades, Velvet and Lace.

LOVELY EVENING GOWNS in Hand-embroidered Jet, Sequin and Fancy Taffetas.

AFTERNOON GOWNS in Artificial Silk in self colours and floral designs.

NEW COAT FROCKS, Paris Model.

COAT SUITS in Tricoline Coating and Repp Cloth.

SPANISH and CHINESE SHAWLS for Evening Wear.

INSPECTION INVITED

ALL PURCHASES SENT CARRIAGE PAID

JAMES M'EWEN & CO.

Ladies' Dress Specialists

PERTH

ladies insured their McEwen's dresses for £200 each. In 1904, the *Telegraph* reported:

> Seldom in the provinces have ladies the chance of examining the very pick of French and English modes as is possible with this old-established and up-to-date establishment; and the very extensive patronage accorded the firm by a very exclusive clientele shows how much this feature of the business is appreciated…Altogether McEwen's this year has even surpassed its usual form - which is no small praise.

Traditionally, the entire gamut of retailers had worked on fairly high profit margins. They had to be sure that they would make sufficient profit eventually to subsidise the credit that they were obliged to extend to their customers. It was quite usual in the eighteenth and nineteenth centuries for customers to haggle over price, although the retailer had the advantage. A shopkeeper could deliberately start the bidding high or match the price to the customer because there were no price tickets on display. Price tickets were considered to be vulgar. Shopkeepers automatically gave upper class customers credit. Their customers accepted this credit as a right, rather than as a privilege. It was a right that they frequently abused. The upper classes would sometimes take years to pay their bills. It has been said that a society lady felt under no pressure to settle her dressmaker's bill until two or three years had passed. This meant that a dressmaker would need a float of three years' income for her business to be viable.

In the 1820s, Elizabeth Grant's family experienced tremendous difficulty in meeting their financial commitments. Their inability to pay their debts forced them to leave Scotland and settle abroad:

Buying drapery on credit, 1897

> A coachmaker, not paid for some repairs done to the carriage at various times, seized it for a debt of £40. He was inexorable; we must pay our bill or lose our carriage. William came to me; I never saw him more annoyed; all our imperials and other luggage seized, like wise…We were much annoyed my brother and I by hosts of unpaid tradesmen, whom it was agreed that I should see, as they were likely to be more considerate with me - I, who could do nothing. The only cross creditor among the crowd was old Sanderson the Lapidary; there really was not much owing to him; a few pounds for setting some of uncle Edward's agates; these few pounds he insisted on getting, and as there was no money to be had he kept a pretty set of garnets he had got to clean…they were set in gold, and though not in fashion then, have been all the rage since. I was thankful to get rid of even one of those unfortunate men, whom I was ashamed of seeing daily at our hotel….

Although she says that she was ashamed, she betrays more than a little irritation at being pressed for payment of 'a few pounds'. She does not really acknowledge the hardship that their unpaid bills might cause.

In the mid-nineteenth century, innovative new retailers like John Anderson began to chip away at the traditional system and turned their backs on offering credit terms. However, many such businesses, department stores in particular, although they refused to offer credit when they were first established, did later institute a customer account system, but these accounts were strictly for the well to do. Anderson sold for cash at fixed low prices and not everyone could afford to take advantage of his terms. People on low incomes often had no alternative other than to avoid shops altogether and buy clothes and household goods from a credit draper or tallyman, who would call on them in their own homes. Credit drapery evolved on the back of the industrialisation of the textile industry. A plethora of manufactured products was becoming available. Credit drapers supplied customers with the goods that they needed, but could not afford to buy outright. Their customers would pay for their purchases in small weekly instalments. Credit drapers built up a sales round and guarded it jealously, visiting customers on a weekly basis to collect repayments. They would try to sell the customer something new before the initial debt was fully paid off. The most successful credit drapers would always keep good accounts 'live'. Even when they had no connection with Scotland at all, credit drapers in England were often known as Scotch Drapers or Scotch Hawkers. This was probably because this particular type of selling was thought to have originated in Scotland.

Just as credit drapery was gathering steam, its very existence was threatened. In the late eighteenth century, the government tried to raise additional revenue by introducing a new shop tax. They hoped to mollify those shopkeepers who would be angered by outlawing peddling at the same time. Such a move would have put an end to credit drapery. The textile manufacturers who supplied the credit drapers were horrified at the prospect of the loss of what had become a very lucrative business. They made strong representation to the politicians and the government was forced to yield to their pressure. The tax changes were abandoned and the credit drapers, together with all other pedlars and hawkers, were free to continue to ply their trade.

Robert Lawson, founder of Lawson's of Dundee, was born in 1828 and, as a young man, worked for many years as a credit draper in the area around Stirling. He was a shrewd businessman and made sure that he set his customers' weekly repayments at a level that each customer could afford, ensuring that he always received full payment for his goods. By 1856, he had enough capital behind him to open a small shop in Stirling.

He still went out on the road, but his customers now had the option of visiting his shop, where they could see a wider range of stock than it was possible for him to bring to their homes. Customers bought goods from the shop on exactly the same credit terms that they were offered in their homes. The shop did well and Robert was soon able to open a second branch in Dundee. In 1872, he sold the Dundee branch to his brother, James. In 1900 the brothers brought the two companies together again as a public company. They had a third branch in Aberdeen as well and a large staff of travelling salesmen.

James Lawson initiated a distinctive staffing policy: Lawson's only employed salesmen who were members of Temperance Societies. His theory was that these men would see it as their mission in life to encourage working men to spend so much money on clothing and household goods that they would have none left to spend on alcohol. Be that as it may, there is no doubt that Lawson's prospered under the leadership of successive members of the family. A hundred years after Robert Lawson opened his first shop in Stirling, Lawson's had grown to a chain of fifteen, employing a staff of 1,100. There were eight branches in Scotland and a further seven in the London area. The shops, whether in London or in more rural areas, all carried much the same range of stock and continued to offer credit trading. In the 1960s, the Dundee branch still recorded almost 99% of its sales as credit transactions. By this time, the salesmen who went out on the road did so in company cars, clocking up as many as five hundred miles in a week and each handled approximately seven hundred individual accounts. However, from the mid-1970s, life became increasingly precarious for any company that was based on the in-house supply of credit, and Lawson's future became uncertain. It was taken over in 1981.

When Kitty Harris's mother was widowed, she was left with eleven children to support and they all had to earn a living as quickly as they could. In the early 1920s, the oldest of the girls started up in business as a credit draper. As soon as she was old enough, Kitty joined her. They were based in Glasgow, but built up a sales round that extended as far as Greenock, Girvan, Dunoon and Rothesay. The whole family would sometimes decamp to Rothesay for three months over the summer and the girls worked from there. Unlike some credit drapers, they were not tied to any one particular supplier and had links with many. In this way, they could offer a huge variety of goods and were free to source whatever their customers wanted. They grew to know their customers very well; some became more like friends than customers. However, they could not afford to forget that they were in business and that their business was selling.

Kitty and her sister let nothing stand in their way. The weather certainly never stopped them from going out on their rounds and even the General Strike failed to stop them in their tracks. With the buses off the road, the sisters simply hitchhiked their way to their customers. In 1935, Kitty bought her very first car. It cost her £100 but, unfortunately, it had no heater. In the winter, her mother made sure that she set off with a blanket tucked around her legs and a hot water bottle strapped to her chest. Kitty's customers would refill the bottle with hot water for her as the day progressed. She relished the freedom that credit drapery gave her. She was never afraid for her personal safety, even when she was carrying money. The whole package suited her admirably, 'I loved driving, I wasn't stuck behind a counter and there was no boss breathing down my neck.' It suited her so much that she carried on working after she married and had children. Kitty continued in business until she was well beyond normal retiral age.

The entire family at the wedding of one of Kitty's sisters

A logical extension of credit drapery was mail order selling. This was particularly popular in rural areas. From the 1920s, mail order companies, such as Littlewoods and Great Universal Stores, published regular catalogues of goods that could be paid for by instalment. Mail order companies appointed local part-time agents to promote the service and collect payments and these agents were given discounts on their own purchases.

From the late nineteenth century, there had been another variation on this theme. Salespeople sold financial credit door to door in exactly the same way as a credit draper sold drapery. The growth in this market was absolutely enormous and remains so to this day. Borrowers bought vouchers or credit cheques that they paid for in small weekly instalments. They could exchange them in any of the shops that were linked to their particular credit scheme. A single cheque could be spent in a number of different shops. The retailer would note the details of each purchase on the back of the cheque and return it to the customer. The customer could use it until its total value had been reached. On the face of it, this was a better system than credit drapery, because it allowed the customer to shop around for the best price and choose from a wider variety of goods. However, rates of interest were high and some borrowers were all too easily sucked into a vortex of spiralling debt. Sheer desperation for ready cash sometimes forced a borrower to redeem a credit cheque for cash on the black market. If they did this, they might only get the cash equivalent of half of the cheque's face value. Of course, the original loan would still need to be repaid in full. 'Provident cheques' dominated this home credit market, especially in the poorer areas of Glasgow and Edinburgh, although they faced some competition from companies such as Caledonian and Bristol. In Scotland today, most people have a debit card or cash card and one or more credit cards. Some have a selection of store cards as well. However, approximately 14% of households still do not have access to a bank account and those on very low incomes continue to obtain credit from private credit companies.

Agnes Smith was an agent for Provident in the Portobello district of Edinburgh from the mid-1950s to the mid-1970s. At that time, it cost ten pounds and ten shillings to buy a ten-pound credit cheque. The customer would pay for it in weekly instalments of ten shillings. If the customer was a married woman, her husband was supposed to sign the documentation for the loan. Customers would frequently be paying up for more than one cheque at a time. There was a two-week period of grace for defaulters, but after two weeks they were blacklisted. Some customers preferred to buy a voucher for a particular shop. Many people used their credit vouchers to buy the new-style package holidays from a designated travel agent. Although Agnes often carried quite large sums of money about with her, she was well known in the neighbourhood and never felt that she was putting herself at risk. Sometimes she would even take her young daughter out with her when she was collecting payments. She made a point of calling for payments on a Friday evening when the men were at home and before their wages were spent. She made about thirty calls in the course of the evening and always carried a large bag of toffee doddles. Her sweeties ensured that the children always eagerly anticipated her visits, although their parents were probably rather less keen to hear her knock at the door.

Chapter 7

Working lives: 1900-1960

At the turn of the last century, shop assistants in Scotland, as elsewhere, worked very long hours for relatively poor wages. In 1893, a Royal Commission on Labour had reported that assistants in bakery shops were working as many as eighty-three and a half hours per week and that even in china shops they often worked as many as sixty-nine and a half hours per week. Nevertheless, working in a shop was seen as a step up from domestic service, factory or manual work and it offered a way of life that was attractive to young people. By the late 1930s, even though the maximum working week for those under the age of eighteen was still set at seventy-four hours, nearly half of all shop assistants in Scotland were less than twenty years of age. But not all shop assistants were young girls without responsibilities. In his autobiography, *Gorbals Doctor*, George Gladstone Robertson recalled a woman he had delivered of her twenty-second child. Just three days after the birth of this baby, she did as she had always done and went back to work, serving in a greengrocer's shop, as if nothing untoward had happened.

Helen Scott and Elizabeth Fernie both began working in their teens. Their experiences could hardly have been more different: Helen Scott spent four years on the Orkney island of Sanday, working in the tailoring business that was owned by William Scott and his son; Elizabeth Fernie went to work at Stobie Taylor's drapery store in the city of Edinburgh.

The Scotts' business interests on Sanday were many and varied: they

C. Garson, butcher, Stromness, c. 1900

owned a tailor's shop, a grocery store which had its own horse-drawn delivery van and a butcher's shop. Helen joined them in May 1919 and worked principally in the tailoring business. She recalled her time there in a short memoir, written in 1993. The Scotts had taken on another young girl at about the same time and she worked mostly in the grocery store. The two girls soon became firm friends. They lived in and were very well looked after by the housekeeper. Helen remembered that she was given a comfortable iron bed all to herself - this was obviously a luxury - and that the housekeeper, who had trained as a cook, would make splendid Saturday evening suppers 'that Mr Scott also shared with the young fellows that had grown up from childhood around him'. Helen wrote of her employer with respect and affection and remembered that he had a special knack of greeting strangers who visited his shops, quickly putting them at their ease.

Mr Scott Junior, 'Young Bill', ran the thriving grocery business. He used his two-horse van to carry hen feed, eggs, poultry, rabbits and game to outlying customers. Soon after Helen arrived, he opened a butcher's shop as well and, in addition to her tailoring work, Helen helped out in the other businesses whenever it became necessary. She drove the pony and float to the bake house for bread, collected egg boxes and delivered hen food. On two occasions, much to the amusement of the old men that they encountered on their way, she and the 'grocery girl' went out on the road. Helen drove the two-horse van around the island while the grocery girl did the selling. By far her most favourite errand was to take the horses to be shod at the smithy, 'No walking for me then. I had to get on their back and do a bit of senseless "show off".' These antics came to an abrupt end after a nasty accident in which she was thrown and badly bruised.

Although Helen only stayed with the Scotts for about four years, she remembered her time with them with 'gratitude and thanksgiving'. They must have been as fond of her as she was of them. Many years later, when she became a widow, she was greatly surprised and somewhat overwhelmed to receive a letter and a cheque from Mr Scott Junior for £100. 'It was surely most kind after a lapse of so many years'.

Elizabeth Fernie began her career at Stobie Taylor when she was just fourteen years old. The two branches, at St Mary Street and the Pleasance, sold all manner of clothing, for men, women and children, at prices substantially lower than those charged by more prestigious city-centre shops, such as those on Princes Street. When she spoke about Stobie Taylor in 1984, Mrs Fernie stoutly defended the two shops and the range and quality of the goods that they sold. Nevertheless, she was not enthusiastic about absolutely everything and could not hide her distaste for the moleskins that Stobie Taylor kept for the miners:

Horse drawn shop van, Orkney, c.1900

> Ah the stench that used tae come offa they moleskins…they were hard-wearing for down the pits…what a smell they were. And we used tae sell navy blue singlets which country people called 'peeweeps'…you could just imagine a white one…it wouldnae last two minutes.

Fourteen-year-old Elizabeth had to learn her trade very quickly indeed:

> The staff were getting called up…into the army, you know, girls got called up too of course…with the result that you were the wee yin when you arrived at fourteen and at sixteen you had become a big one: you were takin' charge of things you know.

> I actually got a very good training in Stobie Taylor…it was a cheap shop, you know, but it didn't sell cheap goods…his mark-up price was very low and he was able tae sell good quality because maybe the rates weren't very high because o' being in the Cowgate. Well, as I was saying, you really did get a very good training. I mean when I look at shop assistants now, I mean, they're just a lot o' old rubbish. I mean, we had tae sell, and I mean, you were told at fourteen that you had tae sell, I mean, when a person came in for something if you didn't have it…well, you sel't them something else, you know that's how you were taught and never to tell them to go to another shop - I mean, that was a mortal sin. You had tae, you know, find something for them. If they wanted a navy blue coat, you made sure that if you only had a red coat, well, they suited red and it was the best colour, it was the best quality you know, you had tae give them all the spiel which I enjoyed actually.

It was all a world away from Orkney and the social niceties of William Scott. The competition in Edinburgh was fierce and Stobie Taylor went in for the hard sell.

Shops and shopping were rapidly becoming big, big business and opportunities abounded for people to break into retailing. Peter Wyper, Duncan McGregor and Bachan Kharbanda all found their particular niche and started businesses that reflected the changes in society.

Peter and Daniel Wyper were champion melodeon players. They came from a large Lanarkshire coal mining family. Peter was born in 1861 and his younger brother, Daniel, was born some eleven years later. Their father had been a miner and the brothers began their working lives in the coalmines too. However, their shared love of music provided them with a way out. The melodeon was a button accordion and it was first manufactured in Germany in the 1820s. It became extremely popular during the latter half of the nineteenth century. Peter and Daniel were accomplished exponents and their musical fame soon spread. They both won many competitions for their melodeon playing and are believed to have played together at a royal command performance for Queen Victoria.

Peter, the elder brother, left the mines first. In the 1890s, he became a sewing machine salesman and then sometime around 1902, he managed to combine business with pleasure and opened a music shop in Cadzow Road in Hamilton. He sold all manner of music-related items: sheet music, musical instruments, gramophones, phonographs, and disc and cylinder records. He also supplied a hire and repair service for musical instruments and gramophones. While he was still working as a miner, his younger brother Daniel rose to prominence as a cornet player in the pit band. Eventually he too left the coalmines to give more time to his music. Daniel led a chequered career. He tried his hand at a variety of money making schemes: he opened and closed a number of second hand goods shops, a fish and chip shop and an ice cream business, but he was most successful as a musician. He played in local dance halls and music halls and also worked for Peter, repairing melodeons and gramophones.

Before the advent of disc records, the brothers recorded cylinders of melodeon music together in the back room of Peter's shop. They issued these recordings under their own record label, Wyper's Empress Records. Later they went on to record a number of 78rpm discs in London for Columbia/Regal Records and their various recordings were all on sale at Peter Wyper's shop.

Duncan McGregor opened the first supermarket in Aberdeen. He was born in a small village near Huntly. His parents worked in the grocery trade and it was in grocery that Duncan found his first job. As soon as he left school he went to work in his uncle's licensed grocery, out in the country at the Glens of Foudland. There was a croft attached to the shop and young Duncan began his long working day at six-thirty in the morning, helping with the animals. He did not finish until at least nine in the evening, when the shop closed. He was an industrious boy and soon assumed total responsibility for the running of the shop as well as continuing to help out on the farm. He received little thanks from his aunt for his trouble and, even though he was a close member of the family, he enjoyed precious few home comforts. Despite the fact that there were many empty rooms in his uncle's house, Duncan had to share a bothy room with Hector, the van man. Duncan and Hector were left to spend one particular freezing winter sleeping in an old railway carriage, while a new bothy room was being built. Such hardship notwithstanding, being licensed, the shop was a convivial place and Duncan worked there quite happily until he felt that the time had come to start a business of his own. He left his uncle and aunt and went into business with his brother, supplying eggs to customers throughout central Scotland. He joined the army in 1940 and saw active service in Africa, Italy and northern Europe. His war experience, which is fully described in his autobiography, *A Desert Rat in Holburn Street*, was traumatic and it left an indelible mark.

After the war, Duncan returned to the Aberdeen area and found work in the grocery trade again. By 1950 he was able to open a grocery shop of his own. 'Trade grew quickly, and I remembered having takings of £200 in a week and thinking I could buy half of Aberdeen'. However, in practice he would have been hard pressed to find the time. It was not until eight years later that he managed to take a break from his normal routine of working from seven in the morning until nine or ten at night, to take a three-day holiday in a pre-fab at Finzean. Duncan nurtured his business well and eventually he bought the shop premises that he had been renting. He also bought a piece of adjoining land so that he was able to extend his shop to twice its original size. In 1962, he took a very deep breath and converted his store from counter service to the new self-service way of food shopping. It was a bold step and his fellow grocers were sceptical. Supermarkets were still in their infancy in Scotland and there were no other self-service groceries in Aberdeen. Initially, his customers were extremely reluctant to put their purchases in the wire baskets as they walked about the store, but they soon accepted the new system and Duncan's initiative paid off: he almost doubled his takings.

Duncan McGregor was never afraid to trust his own commercial instinct. The three-day pre-fab holidays became a thing of the past and, as he proudly recalled, the time came when he was in a position to be able to indulge himself. On one memorable occasion he spent his annual two-week break from business cruising to New York in some considerable luxury aboard the QE2.

After the outbreak of the Second World War in 1939, the working lives of those involved in the retail sector were subject to great change. Some time before war was declared, the government asked shops to release female staff for training in the Women's Auxiliary Territorial Army and as Air Raid Wardens. It was also announced that retailing would not be considered a 'reserved occupation' and that those men who worked in shops would be available for conscription. Once the war began, the opening hours of shops were sharply curtailed. All shops had to close each evening at no later than six o'clock, although they were allowed one late night each week when they could remain open for an extra hour and a half. An ever-increasing number of restrictions began to be imposed on retailing and purchasing.

In September 1939, blackout material became quite literally the new must-have. On the Friday before the war alone, over eight miles of such cloth was sold in the city of Glasgow. Those working in food shops soon had to cope with the demands placed on them by the food-rationing scheme. A similar scheme was soon put into place to cover the sale of clothing. 'Utility' became the new buzzword: utility clothing was intended to be functional and easy care and it was exempt from the wartime purchase tax of 33.3%. However, it was also surprisingly stylish. Without doubt it was the very latest thing and its reputation was enhanced when Norman Hartnell, the couturier, agreed to design a range of utility clothing for a clothing manufacturer. Later in the war, the utility scheme was extended to incorporate the design and manufacture of furniture. Wartime retailers were beset with problems: they had to comply with the myriad wartime regulations, cope with staff shortages and with the diminishing and erratic supply of goods. Inspectors were sent out to make sure that retailers were keeping to the rules. As well as the ration books that people were given for food, everyone received an annual clothing ration book. This did not mean that people did not have to pay for their clothes; it meant that you could not buy an item of clothing unless you could first hand over the necessary number of clothing coupons. In order to buy a dress, you had to proffer eleven coupons. One kind-hearted Glasgow shopkeeper was eventually persuaded to take pity on a bride who did not have enough coupons to cover her wedding finery, only to discover that the seemingly desperate bride was really an undercover inspector. Her misguided kindness cost her a hefty fine.

Many retailers faced the constant worry of bomb damage. In Edinburgh, staff at Jenners joined a fire-watching rota. They kept a constant lookout and a team of four was on duty at the store every weekend. This was not too onerous a duty and they spent much of their time playing table tennis. They slept on bunks in the staff restaurant and were allowed to use the huge Delft bathtub in the director's apartment on the top floor.

In 1942, Hugh Fraser became president of the Cottage Homes, a national charity that supported those who had worked in the drapery trade. Hugh Fraser was only too aware that many former shop owners and shop assistants were experiencing great hardship. Many businesses had been forced into closure and others had been obliged to amalgamate. He launched a special campaign and raised a record £20,000 for the charity's funds.

The Cottage Homes is known today as Retail Trust. It supports those working in the retail industry, those who have retired from it and their dependants. Cottage Homes was founded originally to provide residential care for people who had worked in drapery and its first retirement estate was opened at Mill Hill in London in 1898. There is a Scottish Retail Trust care complex in Glasgow, at Newton Mearns. The name of the charity was changed because it was felt that 'Cottage Homes' no longer fully reflected the work that the charity undertook. Today, in addition to residential care, the Trust offers a wide range of services: legal advice, counselling on a range of issues, financial assistance, day care facilities, respite care and support for carers. Although the charity was founded originally for the support of those who had worked in the textile and haberdashery business, its remit has gradually been extended to encompass those who worked in fashion shops and department stores and ultimately to all sectors of the retail industry.

Sidney Cohen spent the last few years of his life in a flat that is part of the Retail Trust complex at Newton Mearns. As a young man, Sidney had travelled all over America where he worked in a variety of jobs, from bus driver to builder. While working as a builder, he was one of the team that laid the foundations of the Empire State building. Unfortunately, he did not find fame or fortune in America and, after a short while, he returned home to his family in Glasgow. He ran his own costume jewellery business in Glasgow for many years, until it was taken over by Links Warehouse. At this point in his career, he went to work for Links, a large warehouse wholesale business that sold a variety of goods, including drapery. It was this drapery connection that entitled Sidney, as he turned eighty, to apply for a flat in what was known locally as the Crookfur Cottage Homes at Newton Mearns. Throughout his long

Sidney Cohen

retirement, he was an amazingly active man. He was a founder member of Parklands, the health club that was built close to the Cottage Homes. In an unvarying routine, every single morning, until the very last weeks of his life, he swam at the club, exercised on the treadmill and took full advantage of many of the other exercise machines. He would then join a group of friends for a morning game of snooker. He was a wonderful advertisement for the club and they were justly proud of him. On his ninetieth birthday, they presented him with a gold snooker cue and honorary membership of the health club for the rest of his life. Sidney Cohen was fully independent until just the last few weeks of his life, when he moved from his flat to the care facility that operated in the main block of the Cottage Homes. He died in 2000 at the age of ninety-one.

Bachan Kharbanda

Bachan Kharbanda opened the first boutique in Scotland to sell Indian clothes. Bachan came to Glasgow from India as a student in 1954. His father, who had also once been a student in Scotland, was now back in India and working as a Social Education Officer. Part of his remit was to encourage the development of village craft centres. Bachan was particularly interested in this aspect of his father's work and father and son were not slow to recognise the commercial opportunity that it presented. They decided that Bachan should try to develop a market in Scotland for the goods that were being produced by village craft centres in India.

He began, while he was still a student, with a stall in the Barras. Bachan went on to open a shop in the city called 'Outfitters' that he fitted out himself, with the help of a Canadian friend. 'Kohinoor Crafts' soon followed. It opened on Great Western Road in 1956 and was a huge success. It appealed to two different markets: to the young students at the nearby University of Glasgow and to older people who had been in India before or during the war. The older customers were delighted to be able to buy their favourite Indian products in Scotland and the brand of soap that had been supplied to the British Army in India was especially popular. Bachan listened carefully to his customers, young and old, and, whenever possible, he responded positively to their suggestions and requests. He combined a keen business sense with a sharp eye for colour and fashion:

> There was a time when people were wearing a lot of orange here. Then orange was completely dead, but in America it was still going. Then I knew they would be going to wear brown or be wearing dark greens, because I knew automatically what the colour combinations would be - people will like to use some of their old clothing and try to blend it with the new....

Bachan's designs were a fusion of Indian craftwork and Western fashion. His shop on Great Western Road was quite unique. It was a small, multi-purpose bazaar:

> Now we were the first people to introduce boutiques in Britain - there were no boutiques. It was only in my shop that you could buy jewellery, you could buy a skirt, you could buy joss sticks, you could buy bedspreads, you could buy handbags...

However, Bachan was still restless. His Glasgow businesses had worked out extremely well, but he was not entirely happy. He had long wanted to live in Edinburgh. He liked the more traditional feel of the capital city and even the climate on the east coast of the country was more to his taste. He set his mind on yet another new venture and soon found the ideal location. In December 1957, he opened a boutique called Eastern Crafts on Edinburgh's Royal Mile:

> We started advertising from the first day, right on top of the *Scotsman* ...in all the different languages, sometimes Hindi, sometimes Urdu. It always looked funny - in the *Scotsman*, in the corner right at the top, written in Hindi was 'Eastern Crafts'. Then I'd described the shop underneath and that was a great attraction to the public.

Bachan used an old yellow Austin 7 car as an advertising billboard. The brightly coloured vehicle attracted huge attention as it travelled around the city and brought him many new customers. Other cars would follow it in convoy and people would pose alongside it for photographs. The success of Bachan's business was assured and his shop was an Edinburgh landmark for very many years.

Main Street, Newton Mearns, c. 1915

Chapter 8

A brave new world

In the last forty years of the twentieth century there was a new dynamic in retailing. Suddenly, shopping opportunities were omnipresent: at airports, railway stations and motorway service stations, historic homes, art galleries and museums, in hospitals, universities, in city centres and in remote rural locations. The biggest change was the introduction of the American-style shopping mall. At times, it seemed as if a new shopping centre opened almost every day, but in fact more shops closed than opened and the number of retailers and shops in Scotland was on the decline. The largest companies took an even larger slice of the retail market. In 1986, the ten largest enterprises accounted for just over 32% of retail sales in Scotland. By 1996, this figure had risen to over 36% and the independent retailer had to offer the consumer something very different in order to succeed: an innovative product, specialist stock, a unique ambience, value for money. There was also the challenge of a new kind of merchandising as the World Wide Web opened up a worldwide market to the retailers of Scotland.

Main Street, Newton Mearns was bulldozed to make way for Mearns Cross Shopping Centre in the early 1970s. The Glasgow suburb of Newton Mearns was originally a village, with a crossroads and a traditional main street. They both had to go to make way for the new development. Mearns Cross, built by Sir Ian MacTaggart, opened in December 1972 and its management promised that within three months it would have three supermarkets, greengrocers, butchers and bakers, fashion shops, a gift shop, a chemist, a post office and a bank. Customers at the new shopping centre were spared any inconvenience. The 300 feet long mall was fully enclosed and air-conditioned and protected them from rain, wind, snow and even the occasional sunshine. There were two car parks that between them could accommodate 750 cars. This was the brave new world indeed. Mearns Cross has undergone many changes, not least a change of name. A Marks and Spencer food store and an Asda supermarket now anchor 'The Avenue' at Newton Mearns. Natural light has been let in and car-parking facilities extended. Yet more parking spaces will become available shortly and the 60,000,000th customer was expected to cross the centre's threshold in February or March 2002.

Mearns Cross was one of the first of many American-style shopping malls to be built in Scotland in the latter part of the twentieth century. Since 1974, four such malls have been opened in Glasgow city centre alone: the Sauchiehall Street Centre, the St Enoch Centre, Princes Square

and the Buchanan Galleries. They have taken the place of the old Victorian shopping arcades of which only one, the Argyle Arcade, home of the city centre's jewellery trade, still exists. Even though there is some degree of overlap, with a number of national multiples represented in more than one mall, each has a distinctly different style and target audience.

The jewel in the crown is Princes Square. Of the others, the Sauchiehall Street Centre has had an unsettled history and has never really made its mark; the St Enoch Centre, built on the site of the old St Enoch Station, has popular mass market appeal; while the latest addition, the Buchanan Galleries, is pitched a little more upmarket and has the benefit of a John Lewis department store. Princes Square however is something very special. It was originally a four-storey merchant square that was built in 1841. The project's

Princes Square, Glasgow

architects were asked to transform this space into a shopping centre of quality and style and they responded with a design intended to recapture the spirit of the golden age of Glasgow in the 1890s. They adopted a style that reflected the city's former links with the Art Nouveau movement and the Vienna Secession and took as their design theme 'The Tree of

Life'. This theme stems from Celtic and Norse legend and is central to the Glasgow coat of arms. The architects set out to create a new Rialto, a meeting place where people could shop, dine and be entertained. The end result is stunning. When the centre opened in 1987, the first shoppers were astonished to find that the narrow Buchanan Street entrances suddenly opened out to reveal a gracious and spacious five-storey complex, reminiscent of an airy Victorian conservatory. The grand staircase takes the shape of a double helix, with two glass lifts on either side and the two lifts frame the eastern wall of the square, which has been remodelled as a Palladian screen. The whole effect is gloriously theatrical. There are no department stores in Princes Square and each shop unit is relatively small. Disappointingly, even in this rarefied atmosphere, many of the shops are just branches of multiples chains. However, the prevailing ambience does much to enhance their appeal and there are a few independent stores in the centre, such as those selling Scottish gifts and jewellery.

Independent stores do not feature at all at Braehead. The Braehead shopping centre near Paisley cost £285 million to build and is the largest privately-funded waterside regeneration project in the country. It opened to the public in September 1999, much to the consternation of the shopkeepers of Paisley, and houses all the usual multiples, including Marks and Spencer, Sainsbury's, Waterstone's and British Home Stores. In 2001, Ikea opened a massive store within the Braehead complex. At 264,000 square feet, it was the largest new-build store in the United Kingdom and it attracts shoppers from far and wide. In the run up to Christmas 2001, P&O Irish Sea ran special shopping packages from Larne to the Ikea store at Braehead. Scotia Travel has been selling winter shopping breaks to Glasgow in association with Loganair and its flights from Londonderry, the Highlands and Islands. The package features a free lunch at Ikea for those tourists who choose to spend a day at Braehead.

Straiton Retail Park

The Braehead Ikea was the second Ikea store to be built in Scotland. The first opened at Straiton, near Edinburgh, in October 1999 and its opening brought the surrounding road network to a complete standstill. Months of chaos around the Straiton store had been predicted and at the beginning the situation was indeed quite horrendous. Wary of bad publicity, Ikea had offered free delivery to

Ikea, Straiton Midlothian

any customer who travelled to the store by bike or bus in the first two weeks, but consumer curiosity ran very high and there was nothing that the store or the police could do to avert the traffic gridlock.

The Swedish company has stores across Asia, North America and the Middle East, as well as Europe. Ikea is a major player in the global shopping phenomenon that guarantees that shoppers can buy exactly the same thing from a store, decorated and organised in exactly the same way, all over the world. Gap, Borders, Hennes and Mauritz and Disney Store are just a few of the non-UK retailers that now have a strong presence in Scotland's shopping centres. Their numbers are on the increase. So too are the number of mergers, acquisitions and liquidations that have contributed to increasing market concentration, with English-based companies taking an ever larger slice of the Scottish retail market.

The hefty House of Fraser group stems from a shop called Arthur and Fraser's, a drapery store that first opened on Glasgow's Buchanan Street in 1849. By 1959, the Scottish-based company was a department store chain and had grown to such an extent that it was in a strong enough position to buy the prestigious London store, Harrods, and its associated group. Nevertheless, by the mid 1980s, following a protracted period of uncertainty and negotiation, the group succumbed to a takeover bid. Harrods came out of the House of Fraser group in 1984. The remaining stores still operate under their Scottish name, but their management and ownership have passed out of Scottish hands. The House of Fraser is now a London-based company.

Not even the name of William Low's company has survived. It disappeared from Scottish high streets in 1994, when the giant supermarket chain, Tesco, swallowed the firm up. James Low laid the foundation to the Low family grocery business in Dundee, in 1868. Two years later, his twelve-year-old brother, William, joined him in the business and the two brothers entered into a temporary partnership with William Lindsay. In 1879, exactly the same year as the Tay Bridge disaster, twenty-one-year-old William assumed control and William Low & Co. began to take shape. William's brother-in-law, William Rettie, came to work with him and, within approximately twenty years, the two men had built their business into a chain of twenty-six stores. The firm continued to develop and expand under the leadership of an unbroken succession of family members. The first self-service store was opened in 1958 and soon many more were trading in this way. The company was not guilty of resting on its laurels. William Low's ultimate vulnerability was more the result of a general trend in grocery at that time, towards a period of positioning and acquisition by the top five players, than of any mistake on the part of Low's management team. The very largest supermarket chains were battling for supremacy and, while there was still a place for some independent convenience stores and specialist delicatessens, the medium-sized concerns were being squeezed. Five years after Tesco bought the William Low group, the five largest grocery retailers had increased their share of the grocery market by 12%. By 1999, these national giants accounted for over 75% of the grocery market in Scotland.

Ian Mellis, cheesemonger, Edinburgh

A small but vibrant proportion of the remaining 25% comes from the specialists, shops that offer something that the supermarkets just cannot. The central belt is particularly well served. The very best of them are run by enthusiasts, owners or managers who have a detailed knowledge of their particular sector of the food market and who will go to great lengths to source speciality products. Ian Mellis has extraordinary cheese shops in Glasgow and Edinburgh; MacSweens of Edinburgh sells traditional meat and new-style vegetarian haggis that it makes to its own recipe; Fratelli Sarti sells Italian food and wine in Glasgow and Valvona and Crolla, a long-established independent family-run food shop and wine merchant, specialises in the supply of Italian products in Edinburgh.

Benedetto Valvona started the company's first store in 1860 in the Old Town. The company changed its name and location in 1934, when Alfonso Crolla was taken into partnership. Today, the company has a shop and café on Elm Row that is an absolute cornucopia of Italian food and wine. Once over the threshold, the aroma hits you and you could almost

*Valvona &
Crolla, Italian
delicatessen,
Edinburgh*

be in Italy. Italian vegetables are brought directly from the market in Milan, Italian bread is freshly baked and recipe dishes are prepared in their own kitchens to traditional family recipes. Because this is a family business, they can offer the sort of consistent and personalised service that no supermarket could begin to match. Their website puts customers in direct contact with the person who has responsibility for each of the different categories of food or wine that they stock. The greater part of their range is sourced from small artisan suppliers, committed to the production of quality speciality foodstuffs. They carry speciality British cheeses, as well as Italian, and an extensive selection of Scotland's national drink, as well as of Italian wine.

Scotland's national fish has become big business. Even in medieval times, salmon fisheries were valuable possessions and figured in many burgh charters. The Priory of Beauly, in Inverness-shire, and that of Ardchattan, on Loch Etive in Argyllshire, had annual incomes of about £200 in the thirteenth century and, in both cases, this income was derived principally from salmon. When Edward I came to Scotland, early in the fourteenth century, large amounts of salmon were used for his entertainment. Traditionally, preserved salmon was an important constituent of the Scottish diet and when Orkney smoked salmon producer Sutherland Watson's export business was booming in the mid 1960s and he needed to extend his small smokehouse in Kirkwall, the factory building that he chose had actually been used as a fish-drying kiln in the seventeenth century.

There is always a queue of people waiting to be served at the Loch Fyne Oysters' shop at Cairndow. The shop sells locally-smoked salmon, lots of oysters and a great deal more besides. Tourists and locals flock to buy all manner of preserved salmon, fresh fish, seafood, traditionally reared and grass-fed beef and lamb and a variety of other local foodstuffs. John Noble and Andrew Lane started their business, Loch Fyne Oysters Ltd, with an oyster farm on Loch Fyne. In 1980, Noble opened a restaurant on the loch at Cairndow. The menu consisted of Loch Fyne Oysters' own produce, simply prepared and served with a refreshing lack of pretension. Everyone who came to eat in the restaurant wanted to buy fish to take home and so a retail outlet was a natural progression. The company is firmly committed to 'total sustainability'. All the smoked salmon that Loch Fyne Oysters sells bears an ECO label that reinforces the message that the guiding principle of their business is environmental: 'respect for the animal and for its habitat'. But Scotland remains as much a divided society today as it was a century ago and a horribly stark contrast exists between the sumptuous produce available from Loch Fyne Oysters and exotic city centre delicatessens and the pallid, over-processed foods that are stocked by the 'convenience' stores on the poorest Scottish housing estates.

What Every Woman Wants had an annual turnover of £100 million in the late 1980s. In the clothing sector at least, someone got it right. The company dominated the 'value-market', selling mass-produced, fashionable clothing at prices that low-income families could afford. 'What Everys' took Scotland by storm. Customers were getting a good deal and the shops were much beloved. They worked on a rapid turnover, so there was always something new to see. Vera and Gerald Weisfeld bought the excess stock from orders intended for stores such as C & A and sold it for approximately a third of the price that such chains would have charged. The couple could not lose. They began with a single store in a rundown location, a little to the west of Central Station in Glasgow, and built an empire of approximately forty stores spread throughout Scotland and the north of England. The business was sold in 1990 for a staggering £50 million.

In 1999, the mobile phone retailing business, DX Communications, was sold to BT Cellnet for £42 million. It had been founded in Glasgow in 1991 when the mobile phone business was just on the brink of a tremendous expansion. From December 1993, the company opened, on average, a new store every eighteen days and, by 1999, it had a complement of about 140 stores. Mobile phones were 'what everyone wanted' and there was a mobile phone retailer on every street corner. DX Communications was the UK's fastest-growing retailer of 1999 and Richard Emanuel, a founding partner, was named Entrepreneur of the Year. Emanuel was awarded an MBE in the Queen's Birthday Honours List of June 2000, for his services to the telecommunications industry.

Richard Emanuel has just launched a new business called Tomo. The first of what is expected to become a national chain of communication stores has already opened in Nottingham and the second is scheduled to open on home ground in Glasgow in the near future. The company aims to deliver 'an interactive shopping experience' and to make sure that customers understand how to use the equipment that they buy. He is aiming to provide a very high level of customer support. 'Products need to be explained. We aim to put the right device in the right customers' hands'. This might well be a mobile phone with internet access. A growing number of people access information and shop online routinely.

In an article for the *Scotsman*, Professor John Dawson asserted that retailing underpinned the tourist sector:

> Visitors to Scotland carry away with them images of their visit - some of these images are of the shops that they visited, the goods that they bought and the shopping experience they have received.

With the advent of the Internet, this experience is now available online.

People from all over the world can shop in Scotland without ever visiting it and very many do. Scotland has a tremendous advantage in the online shopping stakes. Customers buy with confidence, because traditional Scottish products, such as woollen goods and whisky, have an unrivalled reputation. 'Scotland the Brand' was created as a joint venture for the promotion of Scottish trade, tourism and culture. It is funded by Scottish Enterprise and aims to shape Scotland's image in the global marketplace by developing a national brand identity. The 'Scotland the Brand' device or logo was initiated as a mark of quality that would uniquely identify and authenticate Scottish products and services. A number of Scottish retailers now use the logo and others, such as Marks and Spencer, use it too, to promote Scottish goods sold within their stores.

The 'Scotland The Brand' logo figures prominently on Hector Russell's website. The Hector Russell Kiltmaker Group sells kilts, Highland dress and Scottish souvenirs. Its sister company, The Whisky Shop, specialises in the sale of malts, blends and liqueurs. There is a separate website that caters specifically for the Canadian market and both have been written in a relaxed, conversational tone. They encourage customers to communicate with each other and with the company on two bulletin boards, 'talkaboutkilts' and 'talkabouthectorrussell'. The company also maintains its own newsletter, *Tartan Times*. When you log on, you hear the sound of the pipes, and panoramic views of Edinburgh and Inverness Castles broadcast from web cams installed in Hector Russell's Princes Street and Inverness branches complete the surfer's Scottish experience.

There are many online gateways to Scottish shopping sites. As its name suggests, 'Luxury Scotland' links to the upper end of the market. It lists businesses such as Edinburgh's celebrated jewellery store, Hamilton and Inches, and the countryside shopping opportunity, The House of Bruar. On the A9 between Perth and Inverness, The House of Bruar sells the very best in country clothing as well as food, books and a variety of other goods and much of their range is available online. On site, The House of Bruar is aimed at the leisure shopper and has its own restaurant and children's playground. There is even a picturesque walk on hand and customers are encouraged to use the store as a base for a scenic stroll through the countryside to the Falls of Bruar. The House of Bruar sells cashmere by Johnstons of Elgin. Johnstons itself operates a mill shop and exhibition centre that has become a major tourist attraction with a blend of retailing and tourism that exemplifies the philosophy of 'Scotland the Brand'. Baxters Highland Village at Fochabers does much the same, but on an even larger scale. Visitors to the Baxters extravaganza can learn the history of the company, see some of the original products in the old museum shop, choose from three different restaurants and shop in any of the four speciality shops.

The discount centres have little of this Scottish identity, but they certainly appeal to tourists. They are as much about a day out as they are about bargain hunting. Scotland's largest centre, the McArthur Glen outlet at Livingston, even has an eight-screen multiplex cinema and a health and fitness centre. McArthur Glen comprises a range of international companies such as Gap, Levis, Marks and Spencer, Calvin Klein and Edinburgh Crystal; all selling their surplus stock at prices considerably lower than those charged on the high street. But it is the luxury end of the retail market with which Scotland is most readily associated.

All over the world, Scottish whisky and Scottish cashmere are especially highly prized. There is also a growing resurgence in Scottish jewellery. Hamilton and Inches have recently reversed the general trading pattern and ventured south of the Border to open a second branch in Knightsbridge. In Glasgow, Eric Smith runs an internationally recognised design-led business. Smith is a master craftsman who has won countless awards for his innovative designs. He has been awarded the Freedom of the Worshipful Company of Goldsmiths of the City of London and is a Freeman of the City of London. Nevertheless, he has resisted any temptation to relocate. His business, which has a team of five goldsmiths, is firmly rooted in Scotland. Eric Smith's wife, Yvonne, works with him and is responsible for the buying, the administration and the running of the shop. They began with one small shop in 1974 and, one by one, added three adjoining properties as each became available.

With Eric Smith, Scottish retailing comes back full circle. He is following in the footsteps of generations of renowned Scottish goldsmiths and is a member of the Incorporation of Goldsmiths of the City of Edinburgh and serves as Trade Warden of the Edinburgh Assay Office. New and innovative businesses like Eric Smith's contribute to the buoyancy of the retail sector in Scotland and, despite all consolidation and the fall in the actual number of shops, Scotland's shoppers now enjoy an unprecedented level of choice in consumer goods and style of shopping.

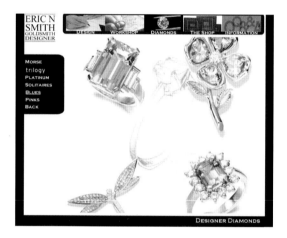

DESIGNER DIAMONDS

Bibliography

Further reading

Baren, Maurice. *How it all began up the High Street*. Michael O'Mara, 1996

Crampsey, Bob. *The King's grocer*. Glasgow City Libraries and Archives Publications, 1995

Davis, Dorothy. *A history of shopping*. Routledge & Kegan Paul, 1966

Dawson, John. *Future patterns of retailing in Scotland*. The Scottish Executive Central Research Unit, 2000

Ewan, Elizabeth. *Townlife in fourteenth century Scotland*. Edinburgh University Press, 1990

Finlay, I. *Scottish gold and silver work*. Strong Oak Press, 1991

Fraser, W. Hamish. *The coming of the mass market 1850-1914*. Macmillan, 1981

Grant, Elizabeth. *Memoirs of a Highland Lady*. Canongate Classics, 1988

Howe, Stuart. *William Low & Co.: a family business history*. Abertay Historical Society, 2000

Keay, John *and* Keay, Julia, *eds. Collins encyclopaedia of Scotland*. Collins, 1994

Ketteringham, Lesley. *The daybook of William MacDonald, Merchant of Lairg 1812 - 1818*. Lairg History Society, 2000

Lancaster, Bill. *The department store: a social history*. Leicester University Press, 1995

Lynch, Michael. Scotland: a new history. Pimlico, 1991

Lynch, Michael, *ed. The Oxford companion to Scottish history*. Oxford University Press, 2001

Lynch, Michael, Spearman, Michael *and* Stell, Geoffrey, *eds. The Scottish medieval town*. John Donald Publishers Ltd, 1988

McGregor, Duncan. *A desert rat in Holburn Street*. Ardo Publishing Company, 1994

Mair, Craig. *Mercat cross and tolbooth*. John Donald Publishers Ltd, 1988

Marwick, Sir James David. *List of markets and fairs now and formerly held in Scotland*. Royal Commisioners on Market Rights and Tolls, 1890

Moss, Michael *and* Turton, Alison. *A legend of retailing: House of Fraser*. Weidenfeld and Nicolson, 1989

New Lanark village store and the development of the co-operative movement. New Lanark Conservation Trust, 1993

Osborne, Brian D. *The last of the chiefs: Alasdair Ranaldson Macdonell of Glengarry, 1773-1828*. Argyll Publishing, 2001

Wordsworth, Dorothy. *Journals of Dorothy Wordsworth, 2v*. Macmillan, 1941

Online reference sources

Scottish Book Trade Index (SBTI)
http://www.nls.uk/catalogues/resources/sbti/index.html

Statistical Accounts of Scotland
http://edina.ac.uk/StatAcc/

Index

NEXT
Evans
BURTON
BRANTANO
WHSmith
COSTA COFFEE
adams
SPORTS SOCCER
mothercare world
DOROTHY PERKINS
principles
LAURA ASHLEY
THE OFFICERS CLUB
Dixons
NEW LOOK